1980

Early Childhood Education

An Overview

P9-ASN-774

Early Childhood Education

An Overview

Loraine Webster
University of South Dakota

and

Raymond M Schroeder
University of South Dakota

Princeton Book Company, Publishers
Princeton, New Jersey

This book is dedicated to our respective children, all of whom have long since left the period of early childhood, but who taught us much along the way.

Grateful acknowledgment is made for the use of photographs as follows: Verlyn Haahr (cover, pages 1, 9, 19, 37, 49, 59, 65, 68, 72, 73), Sharon Waite (pages 20, 64, 71, 73, 77, 83, 85, 99), and the University of South Dakota (pages 15, 42, 56, 94, 95, 97, 107). Loraine Webster supplied the photographs on pages 22, 67, 81, 88.

Preface

Mrs. Anderson had just deposited her youngest child Mary, age three, at a private nursery school operated by a church in the immediate neighborhood of her home. It was a convenient, although fairly expensive, arrangement. Her two older children John and Jennifer, ages nine and six respectively, were at their elementary school which also was within walking distance. So, for the next three or four hours she was free, as she told her friends, "to do some of the things I want to do, just because I want to do them." However, as she drove away from the church, she felt some mild uneasiness and just a twinge of conscience. Neither John nor Jennifer had attended nursery school. The Andersons felt they could not afford it when the older children were "preschoolers." Now Mrs. Anderson wondered to herself if Mary was better off, if the experiences at the school, which was considered a very good one, were really valuable enough to warrant the expense, and, if so, should she and her husband have sacrificed a bit and made sure that the older children also had the advantages of the nursery school experience.

But she didn't really think so. The Andersons maintained an attractive, comfortable home. Children's books, and other good literature, were available. Together, they took the children on fun trips, and always provided them with many educational games and toys. And there was play apparatus both indoors and out. No, she told herself, it was a pretty good environment that she and her husband provided for their children. However, even this self-assurance did not quiet her misgivings, because with such an excellent home environment, did Mary need the nursery school in addition? Were little children better off at home with their mothers, and should parents be entirely responsible for their offspring's educational experience and environment in the years before they started formal schooling? One of her friends was quite sharp in her criticism of parents who "turn their youngsters over to the custodial care of private nursery schools. If children really need whatever it is they get at these places, then let the public schools provide it at taxpayers' expense; then everybody can get rid of their kids at age two or three." This rebuke annoyed Mrs. Anderson, and yet at the same time, it placed her on the defensive. "I don't think I'm being terribly selfish," she told her husband, "because I'm using the time to do many helpful and needed things, but at times I develop quite a guilt complex."

Interestingly enough, on this particular morning she was helping at a rummage sale whose proceeds were to go to a nonprofit day care center where working mothers could leave their children all day at very little cost. On this same morning, Mrs. Smith had left her own two toddlers at this very same day care center. But as Mrs. Smith and her husband drove on to their respective jobs, Mrs. Smith was smitten by neither conscience nor the misgivings which had bothered Mrs. Anderson. She knew that her children would be well cared for through the day. They would have an appetizing and nutritious lunch, a nap in the afternoon, and the whole eight hours would be a pleasant and prosperous time for them. So, instead of feeling concern or guilt, Mrs. Smith breathed a short prayer of thanksgiving for the existence of the center which took such wonderful care of her children while she worked to supplement the family income.

Although Mrs. Smith and Mrs. Anderson are imaginary characters, their contrasting reactions might be shared by some of the hundreds of thousands of real Mrs. Andersons and Mrs. Smiths who day after day leave their children at not only day care centers, but at a variety of other agencies for young children. Some of these are commercial ventures, some are government or foundation supported, some are research oriented or experimental, a few have been established to espouse some cause or educational theory, and some are benevolent, simply trying to provide help where help is needed.

While they vary in origin to some extent, and certainly a great deal in quality and effectiveness, all these institutions have one thing in common. They exist to somehow serve the needs of young children. Together they constitute a broad, sprawling, hard-to-define sector of education in American society called "early childhood education."

In the pages which follow Dean Schroeder and Dr. Webster have brought together the major elements of this fascinating development. Obviously, such a short treatment as this cannot be all-inclusive. Yet the coverage, while admittedly brief, does include a sharp, concise discussion of the background, theory and purposes, types of institutions, research and experimental efforts, and the principal contributions of the people who have lent their best thinking and efforts to the field.

Most importantly, the broad issues which must be faced by both professionals and the society which supports their efforts are isolated and sharpened as focal points for consideration.

W.K. Beggs, Dean Emeritus
COLLEGE OF EDUCATION, UNIVERSITY OF NEBRASKA

Contents

Chapter 1

INTRODUCTION TO EARLY CHILDHOOD EDUCATION

In the last decade and a half a broad new area of education has dramatically emerged known as early childhood education, a title covering a variety of programs and schools for young children. The growing interest in the education and development of young children may be readily apparent to the most casual observer, but the reasons underlying it may not be so obvious. Part of the explanation goes back to the early 1960s. The federal legislation of this period, designed to help eliminate poverty in America, had important implications for education, as did the civil rights movement. Early childhood education was particularly affected.

Briefly, some of the key reasons for the growth of early childhood education are:

1. New attention given to the educational needs of the disadvantaged, especially minority groups.

2. Experimental programs made possible by foundation and government grants.

3. Additional research into learning patterns and needs of the young child.

4. More working mothers.

1

What, then, is early childhood education and what is included under this umbrella term? Why is there so much furor over child development and early childhood education? What are the purposes? Are there quality early childhood programs available? What are some of the educational implications?

These are indeed broad opening questions with which to deal, but an examination of them is important in achieving understanding of early childhood education.

Defining Early Childhood Education

When educators speak of early childhood education, they usually mean education for children from ages two through eight. However, children are learning constantly from birth and a tremendous, probably incalculable, amount of learning takes place before educators ever see them in a school setting. With this in mind, there have been experiments on teaching infants. One such experimental project was the Infant Education Project in Washington, DC. In this program, babies were tutored in their homes until age three with the result that the infants tested at age three did significantly better than the control group of nontutored infants on picture, vocabulary, and perceptual tests (1, pp. 17-18). Another infant stimulation program has been conducted at the University of Florida, using mothers to teach their babies. Here, too, marked gains were noted (1, p. 8). These are but two of many that could be cited.

The recent interest in schools for the very young has given rise to a great variety of programs, and new ones are being added constantly. There are day care programs, Head Start programs, Montessori schools, and many kinds of kindergartens and nursery schools, both public and private. Some of these are parent-cooperative nursery schools and kindergartens. There are laboratory nursery schools and kindergartens affiliated with universities and colleges. There are many parochial or church sponsored schools. There are play groups, organized play schools, and home-based programs that work with preschool children and parents; Home Start is a federally funded program in the latter category. A recent development, home programs for preschool handicapped children, is growing rapidly due to P.L. 94-142 which requires that all handicapped children be provided with an individualized educational program (IEP) that gives them the same educational opportunity other children have. This, according to the federal legislation, must begin in the preschool period. More will be said about this particular law in a later chapter, since it is having such a large impact on early childhood education.

In a rapidly expanding trend toward commercial ventures in early education, the franchised nursery schools and day care centers are making an appearance throughout the United States. These are so new it is difficult to evaluate their worth, but they are growing in number. In spite of all these programs, many of them privately sponsored and operated, early education is still not available to the vast majority of very young children. Although kindergartens were established in the United States in the middle of the nineteenth century, a few states still do not provide kindergarten as a part of their publicly-supported school systems. Some five year olds do not have the opportunity to attend a public kindergarten, and others have only a brief, limited kindergarten experience. Many children have no opportunity for any type of prekindergarten experiences. We must conclude that, although there is extensive current activity and interest in the area of early childhood education, there is still much to be done.

Early childhood education extends through the first three years of elementary school, so we find ourselves dealing with the primary grades as well. Perhaps some day in the not-too-distant future separate schools or units covering the entire span of early education from ages three to eight will be more common than they are at present.

Why The Furor?

Although education for very young children has had a long history, an important reason for the current excitement is the unprecedented growth of opportunities for early childhood education. Much new knowledge has been acquired in recent years, but probably the one most influential movement has been the federal government's program for disadvantaged preschoolers, Operation Head Start, which was started in 1965. This provided an impetus to early childhood education that did not exist before. Much new research and many experimental programs have followed in the wake of Operation Head Start. Some of the earliest research indicated that Head Start was not an unqualified success. In fact, the Westinghouse study (2), one of the first major studies to evaluate the effectiveness of Head Start, found that academic gains were negligible. Children entering public school from Head Start showed a small advantage over peers, but the gains were not maintained. In a year or two the children who had not participated in Head Start caught up with and often surpassed the Head Start children in academic achievement. In view of this study and others, the Follow Through Program was instituted in 1968 so that Head Start gains made in the preschool years could be maintained. Follow Through provides special help for disadvantaged children through the third grade. Both Head Start and Follow Through have focused attention on the young child and, as a result, the public now realizes that the disadvantaged child is not the only child in our society who can profit from early schooling.

Purposes

What is the point of early childhood education? What will be accomplished by it? Why is it needed?

One important purpose of early education is socialization and enculturation.

> Socialization is the process of the individual's interaction with others in the human group. Hand in hand with the concept of socialization goes the process of enculturation. Enculturation takes place within the socialization process, as the individual is fitted into his culture by accepting as his own the norms, values, and attitudes of the groups with which he interacts (3, p. 13).

For a long time in the United States institutions other than educational ones largely socialized the young. The family, primarily, inducted the very young child into the ways and mores of the society. Often, this was an extended family including grandparents, aunts, uncles, and cousins all living together or in close proximity. The church formerly played a much larger role in the young child's training. Although the family is still vital to the child, for a variety of reasons, its responsibility and those of other social institutions has become more and more the responsibility of the school. This additional responsibility may not have been assumed by educators voluntarily, but rather seems often to have been imposed on schools. This larger goal of socialization assumes even more importance when it is seen as a way of equalizing opportunities for disadvantaged children, particularly those of minority groups. The way to success in our society has traditionally been through education. The poor child was to improve himself through education and be started on the successful climb up the ladder. In reality, those children from seriously deprived and culturally limited backgrounds are seldom able to overcome their handicaps well enough to enter the mainstream of American society. Although some ethnic groups today are rebelling vigorously against middle-class practices and values, the culture of the dominant class is still indisputably the most accepted pattern in American society. Americans do have the desire to help the less fortunate, and this wish for equal opportunity seems almost second nature to us. Our sense of fair play is offended by the realization of how very unfair the educational system has been. Part of the purpose of preschool training is to really bring about some equalization. That is what Head Start, and other compensatory programs, have tried to do.

Within this larger goal of socialization and enculturation, another purpose receiving more and more attention is intellectual development. Young children learn so rapidly that some educators now feel we should utilize this vital learning period for optimum academic development. This is a controversial area, since there are still those who feel academic learning has no place in preschool education. These people believe the child should be allowed to develop naturally, à la Rousseau, and to push him into earlier "book-learning" is cruel and unnecessary. He will learn more and faster if he just follows his own bent. Those opposed to this point of view say children today are far more sophisticated and knowledgeable than they were in years past. They have been exposed to the mass media, particularly television, since birth. They have had a virtual barrage of words, spoken and printed, hurled at them from all sides. They are more than ready to engage in translation of our letter and number codes, the symbols so necessary in our modern existence. Those espousing this point of view argue that, rather than pushing the child, it is stimulating him and preparing him for a more successful school career. It enables him to live a fuller life and helps him build on a sound foundation. The television series "Sesame Street" has operated on the premise (apparently with quite a bit of success) that the child is ready at an earlier age for many more symbolic learnings than we have offered him in the past.

A final goal we should examine is perhaps most important. Shouldn't all schools exist to help students live more satisfying, richer lives? Education should be a pleasurable experience. Little children, particularly, should enjoy school and acquire positive attitudes toward all later schooling. Taking a very pragmatic stance, schools should teach us to live. The quality of life in the United States has been a matter of great concern in recent years. One needs to look long and hard at all our schools as vehicles for improving the quality of life; and if schooling begins at age three or four, this is where one should look first. A happy positive initial experience for children will carry over into later periods.

Quality Of Early Childhood Programs

So often in the past programs for very young children have been thought of as simply baby-sitting services provided for the convenience of parents. Are all early childhood education programs actually fulfilling the excellent goals outlined above?

To answer this honestly and fairly it must be said there are not nearly enough schools for young children to begin to attain these goals; and secondly, the quality of programs varies tremendously. The best are superb, but the poorest may often be worse than no school at all. The range is great. If this question is interpreted as a query as to the function early education is actually filling in our society, again there is no single answer. Often, preschools and day care centers are simply providing custodial care for children; but day care centers are being upgraded and many have fine educational programs to offer. Again the range is wide. Even with acknowledged weaknesses, there is a constant improvement as more and better programs come into being. Many educators in the field have great hope that in the near future all early childhood education may fulfill the purposes outlined earlier.

Implications For Education

The last question posed at the beginning of the chapter was: "What are some of the implications for education?" This might be partially answered by the following statement: the concern and interest in early childhood education should result in

1. More and better educational programs,

2. Attention to improved home conditions,

3. More attention to research in the area of early childhood,

4. Increased interest and concern on the part of the entire populace.

History

The entire history of early childhood education cannot be covered in one brief book, but a few highlights should be mentioned. The kindergarten concept and the establishment of the first kindergarten is one of them. A German, Friedrich Froebel, who lived from 1782 to 1852, has become known as the "Father of the Kindergarten." He called his school a "garden of children." He saw play activities as a vehicle for learning. From this, much of the kindergarten curriculum we know has evolved, such as painting and other art activities, clay modeling, singing, dancing, dramatizations, and stories. Froebel was a religious mystic and many of his ideas were not accepted at the time because of his personality. Yet, with the mysticism and symbolism taken away, many of his ideas had practical value and are still used widely. For example, he said that seating children in a circle would help each child identify himself as part of his own little society or social group. This kind of thinking is not difficult for us to accept. Everything done in Froebel's kindergarten was to make the child feel closer to God and to fellow man. His original kindergarten was a school for children of three to six, so it did encompass a greater age span than do present American kindergartens. Froebel's influence has been extremely important, too, in establishing the comfortable, easy atmosphere usually found in schools for young children. There is a freer feeling and less rigidity here than in many later school rooms. That we think of classrooms for young children as happy, attractive places is largely due to Froebel.

In seventeenth and eighteenth century America, primary schools for children from four to seven existed in New England. Some were private, but in Boston, that educational stronghold of our early history, such schools were eventually provided at public expense. Many other larger towns in New England also provided primary schools or reading and writing schools for very young children. Along with these kinds of schools was one imported from England, the Dame School. The dame in the Dame School was a housewife, often a widow needing income, who took very young children into her home and, while doing housework, taught them their letters and the rudiments of reading.

All these early American schools had a serious emphasis on scholarship and academic learning. Of course, they also emphasized, with great vigor, religious training. As we would expect from the Puritans, learning the answers in the catechism was as important as learning to read and write. After all, the whole reason reading was so vitally necessary for them was to enable each individual to read the Bible and other religious material. These schools were not the cheerful pleasant kindergartens of a later day. It is interesting to note that many children under seven learned to read in our colonial period. A later generation was to decide that somehow it was either impossible or educationally unsound to teach children to read at such an early age, and only now are we beginning to realize anew that some children are quite ready to read at five or earlier.

The kindergarten, as started by Froebel in Germany, was brought to the United States in the middle of the nineteenth century. The first American kindergarten, which was located in Wisconsin, was a German transplant completely, including the language. (4, pp. 337-339). The first public kindergarten was started in St. Louis in 1873.

Enthusiasm has been exhibited for various early childhood movements at different times throughout American history, but not until the twentieth century were substantial gains made. Nursery schools and day care centers were started in the twenties and thirties, but got their greatest impetus during World War II. With large numbers of women in the labor force, there had to be child care arrangements to accommodate working mothers. After the war, the interest in programs for preschool children lagged again in the fifties. Nursery schools of this period were only for the most affluent.

The sixties brought about some remarkable changes in attitude toward early childhood education. The federal poverty program and Head Start have already been mentioned as influential. Large numbers of working mothers have created anew the need for quality child care programs. In addition some of the most important research in the field occurred during the sixties. These research findings have affected educators profoundly and much that has been accomplished in early childhood education has been the result of this research. Also, much will continue to be learned from the many specific and experimental programs that have been and are being developed in this dynamic area. We shall examine some of these developments in the following two chapters.

References

1. *Preschool Breakthrough: What Works in Early Childhood Education.* Washington, D.C.: The National School Public Relations Association, 1970.

2. Westinghouse Learning Corporation. *The Impact of Head Start: An Evaluation of the Effects of Head Start Experience on Children's Cognitive and Affective Development.* Athens, Ohio: Ohio University, 1969.

3. King, Edith W., and Kerber, August. *The Sociology of Early Childhood Education.* New York: American Book Co., 1968.

4. Hildebrand, Verna. *Introduction to Early Childhood Education.* New York: The Macmillan Co., 1976.

SUPPLEMENTAL REFERENCES

1. Hess, Robert D., and Croft, Doreen J. *Teachers of Young Children.* Boston: Houghton Mifflin Co., 1975.

2. Hymes, James L. *Teaching the Child Under Six.* Columbus, Ohio: Charles E. Merrill Co., 1974.

3. Braun, S. J., and Edwards, E. P. *History and Theory of Early Childhood Education.* Belmont, California: Wadsworth Publishing Co., 1972.

4. Weber, E. *The Kindergarten: Its Encounter With Educational Thought in America.* New York: Teachers College Press, 1969.

Chapter 2

REVIEW
OF RESEARCH

Anyone wishing to become acquainted with the field of early childhood education must know about the research and theories of at
least the most important leaders in the field. We can examine only a few
of the most notable ones here. However, we want to point out that many
individuals are engaged in research and numerous fine programs exist at
the local level which are not well known. The dynamic is so broad and
covers so much territory that only time will uncover the more significant
of these contributions.

Bloom

Some of the best known work to date has been done by Benjamin
Bloom. Bloom published a book called *Stability and Change in Human
Characteristics* (1) which is highly regarded and widely quoted. Bloom's
writing is significant because, along with his contemporaries, he has led us
to accept some rather startling new ideas, and to look at their implications
for future education. His studies show that the greatest intellectual
development takes place in the years of early childhood. To be more specific, according to Bloom 50 percent of the total intellectual development of
an individual has already been attained by four years of age, and by age

eight the child has gained another 30 percent of his total intellectual development. Hence, if intelligence can be viewed as a developmental trait, then the greatest amount of development takes place by age four, before the child has started formal schooling, and it has almost reached its zenith two or three years after he has started school. Since the greatest proportion of intellectual development is gained in these early years of life, Bloom also contends that early intervention can stimulate and increase mental growth or intelligence. This is a rather startling idea, and it seems almost diametrically opposed to what traditional education practices have been. It seems somewhat out of balance for educators to devote almost all of their efforts to the last 30 percent of intellectual development.

Hunt

Another name of importance is J. McVicker Hunt (2). In Hunt's work, the idea of fixed intelligence has been discarded in favor of a more flexible, developmental concept—one that is particularly susceptible to stimulation in the preschool years. Hunt sees environmental influences in these years as vital to the cognitive development of the child. Hunt would agree that intellectual development can be greatly strengthened in these early years; and, if this is successfully accomplished, we can produce a population with substantially improved intellectual capacities. Hunt actually has reinterpreted the idea of intelligence and is concerned with what he terms the "problem of the match" (2, p. 280). In other words, children must be given tasks matching their mental capabilities. A child must be ready and able to cope with intellectual challenges; and, if offered certain tasks too early or too late, he will not perform in an optimum manner. He also implies great attention to individual differences in each child. Hunt's research indicated a strong link between poor and culturally deprived children and the failure of such children in school. His work has been influential in the establishment of many experimental early intervention programs, including Head Start.

Bruner

Jerome Bruner, whom we shall return to later in another context, published a book called *The Process of Education* (3) that has become very famous. In this work Bruner postulated that any subject could be taught to a child of any age, provided it was properly structured and presented in a manner commensurate with the interests and existing knowledge of the child. In other words, subject areas that we have traditionally considered only within the realm of upper grade children or even high school students may very properly be taught at much earlier ages. It is all a matter of how the material is structured and presented. Bruner has done extensive study with young children to determine more about how children learn and how children approach problem solving at different ages. His findings indicate that the stimulus-response theory is the most applicable to very young children. As children leave the period of infancy Gestalt theory comes into play most frequently—that is, the internalizing of a whole pattern of thought at once. The very young child in his first few years can only deal with one aspect of his environment at a time. With increasing maturity the child is less distractible and can handle more complex information and ideas.

Bruner suggests that intellectual growth must be understood through "psychological mechanisms", but he also notes it is difficult to make generalizations because the cultural background of the individual is a hard-to-define variable in learning. The cultural factor makes it difficult to understand an individual child's motivation. It is not always easy to discern what drives a child to achieve a certain goal.

Bruner's work on structuring appropriate subject material (organizing concepts) into manageable steps for different ages has had an effect on educators at all levels. His rather elaborate theory of the sequential development of learning will be discussed later.

Bereiter And Engleman

During the period from 1965 to 1975 many early intervention programs were instituted. Numerous scholars and researchers implemented programs designed to put into practice the ideas proposed by Bloom, Hunt, and others.

On the basis of this earlier research, Carl Bereiter and Siegfried Engleman speculated that disadvantaged children are already too far behind their more privileged peers in first grade to ever catch up. They argued that such children could only fall further behind as they proceeded through school. With this in mind, Bereiter and Engleman started an academic preschool in Champaign, Illinois, and it is often cited as an example of what can be done to stimulate cognitive development among language-handicapped preschoolers. Bereiter and Engleman believed direct, forceful teaching of the material they needed to learn to catch up with their more advantaged contemporaries was the solution to their educational problems. Working under these premises, these two innovators set up experimental classes which concentrated heavily on language, reading, and math. Very definite goals were set. In reading, methods of word attack, blending, letter names and recognition, alphabetical order, and, finally, word recognition are all to be mastered. In language, the child should be able to reason and deduce orally, broaden vocabulary, understand opposites, and other word relationships. In math, children learn to count (not only forward but backward) as well as learn the symbols for plus, minus, and equal. Verbal skills were emphasized because cultural deprivation was viewed primarily as language deprivation. However, they also concentrated on counting and number concepts. All this was done in a structured, businesslike fashion with a student-teacher ratio of five-to-one. The children were kept so busy "working" at a rapid pace, with much reinforcement of desired behavior, that there was little of the free play and unhurried atmosphere often equated with nursery schools. The work has been notably successful, and the first experimental groups in the program made sizeable gains in I.Q. and achievement. At this time Bereiter is no longer involved, but Engleman and others have made a great impact; because of the demand for their techniques and materials they are training teachers in their methods. Engleman is now working at the University of Oregon with Wesley Becker and the E-B, or Engleman-Becker, materials are utilized in a variety of disadvantaged areas. Their program materials, known as DISTAR, provide the model for many Head Start and Follow Through programs. When the original program, instituted for black children from disadvantaged homes, was evaluated, the data indicated these preschool children made a seven point gain in I.Q., and their performances in reading and arithmetic were comparable to children at the first or second grade level (4, pp. 124-129). Later research showed even larger gains in I.Q. (4, pp. 126-127).

With its total emphasis on cognitive development, particularly in the remediation of language deficits, this program has been a radical departure from conventional early childhood programs. However, as this material and teaching approach have been more widely used, the spectacular gains initially evidenced do not seem so impressive, and there have been many reservations expressed about this "pressure-cooker" type of teaching for young children. Another concern involves the transition from E-B to more conventional teaching styles. Some students experience considerable difficulty in making the necessary transition.

Some parents have objected to their children being "conditioned." Teachers in some Follow Through schools have objected to the teaching techniques and materials they have been required to use. These issues are clarified in a Curriculum Study Report done in schools on the Rosebud Sioux Indian Reservation in South Dakota where DISTAR has been the Follow Through model. The concerns listed under language arts "Areas for Improvement" are typical of those found throughout the report.

Concentration on one type of material and teaching style throughout the Follow Through years creates numerous difficulties in students adapting to different approaches in grades 4, 5, and 6. Examples offered were lack of experience with large group activities and lack of opportunity to work independently.

E-B appears to be an emotionally charged, highly controversial topic at St. Francis. Some teachers are either strongly in favor or strongly against the program. This inevitably leads to lack of understanding between the two groups.

There are strong feelings upon the part of some DISTAR teachers that they don't have the freedom to teach as they wish. Teachers function as aides, always subordinate to the program with supervision being unnecessarily close.

There is a very apparent lack of continuity and coordination between Follow Through and the upper grades. As one upper grade teacher stated, "Teachers have to know what has gone before, what has been taught and how."

In the language arts area, specifically, DISTAR does not apparently provide adequate experience in spelling, handwriting, and the creative use of language.

Teaching aides need assistance in learning how to work effectively with children in other ways than that prescribed by DISTAR (5, pp. 7, 8).

In spite of the controversy that has arisen about the DISTAR program and materials, Engleman and his coworkers have made their mark in the area of early childhood research.

Deutsch

Another notable worker in the area of early education is Martin Deutsch. Deutsch, while on the faculty of New York University, began in the early sixties to work primarily in New York's Harlem schools. He studied and worked with children in prekindergarten classes through third grade. Deutsch has concentrated on skill building in five areas of deficit identified as language, visual perception, concepts, auditory perception, and lack of positive self-image. In his early education project programmed instruction was extensive. Parents were actively involved in the program, holding regular meetings with him to learn how to help their children make more progress at home. These parent meetings also served as social outlets and learning experiences for adults. Many other experimenters have also leaned heavily on parental help (6, pp. 381-384).

Deutsch made the attainment of a positive self-image one of the main goals in his project. He has used many interesting means for accomplishing this, apparently with considerable success. This may not seem terribly important for the middle-class child, but disadvantaged children may be tremendously handicapped before ever entering school because they feel worthless and of no importance, completely insignificant to anyone.

Deutsch's research has attempted to diagnose children's cognitive deficiencies and prescribe the appropriate remedial treatment. He even developed an instrument called a "Deprivation Index," designed to measure the extent and type of deprivation present in individual children (7, p. 306).

Klauss And Gray

Researchers from Peabody College in Tennessee have also done some interesting work. After some earlier experimental efforts, Susan Gray and associates devised a program in which they studied some eighty children in Peabody's Demonstration and Research Center for Early Education. DARCEE was their acronym, and this program still is known as the DARCEE model. Klauss and Gray worked with black, urban children in Nashville as well as with rural children. The Peabody Program was, and is, an eclectic one built around units or central themes. Interestingly, the first unit is based on the child and, as in the Deutsch program, positive self-concept is stressed. Later the child expands his interests to include family, home, neighborhood, and city. Behavior shaping by immediate reinforcement using both tangible and intangible rewards is an important aspect of the Peabody Program, as it is with most of the others. The program also includes parent participation. It uses materials traditionally considered appropriate for young children such as puzzles, paint and crayons, games, and rhythm instruments, but there is also a systematic concentration on language and concept development. After considerable testing, it was reported that the project resulted in positive and significant cognitive gains for the children in the experimental group. One important conclusion reached by the researchers was that the earlier educational intervention could take place, the greater the gain that could be expected. They also stated that the greater the educational deprivation, the more chance there was of effective intervention and compensation (4, pp. 295-296). An outcome of this early work in furthering language development at Peabody College is the widely disseminated Peabody Language Development Kits for the preschool and primary levels. A new Peabody kit for three-to-five year olds has very recently been developed. This latest kit is called PEEK for Peabody Early Education Kit.

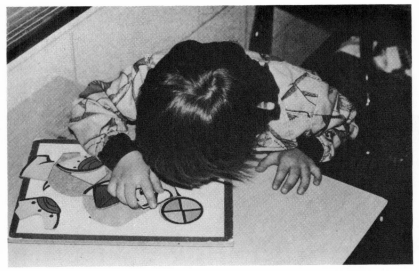

The Peabody program utilizes "traditional" materials such as puzzles.

Weikart

David Weikart has been an active researcher in early childhood compensatory education programs. He has explored the question of whether early intervention can make a real difference in several studies.

Weikart's first evaluative work was the Perry Preschool Project, which he began in 1962 in Ypsilanti, Michigan. The Perry Preschool curriculum offered varied cognitive, affective, and social experience, and it included weekly home visits. Parents and children worked with staff members during these home visits. When compared to a control group, the children from the Perry Preschool did make gains in I.Q.; and after follow-up work of several years' duration, it was determined that children from the program had a less difficult school experience than children from the control group (8, pp. 24-26).

Later Weikart wanted to discover if different types of early childhood programs might be more or less effective with disadvantaged children. Three quite different programs were started. One was a highly structured academic program very similar to the Bereiter and Engleman curriculum.

A second was based on the theories of Piaget. (Incidentally, this second curriculum resulted in an interesting book called *The Cognitively Oriented Curriculum* (9) which describes the Piagetian curriculum as interpreted by Weikart and his fellow workers.) The third curriculum was a traditional early childhood program including active play, stories, and conventional creative activities. All three curricula included home visits and work with parents.

The first results of this comparison study indicated that all three groups made gains similar to the earlier Perry Preschool Project. No one of the three was significantly superior. Long range results are still to be evaluated. Most or all of the longitudinal studies done thus far have shown that children who made quite good initial gains tend to level off and even drop behind peers again after several years.

Karnes

Merle Karnes is another researcher deeply involved in early childhood education. Coincidentally, she did some of her work at the University of Illinois at the same time as Bereiter and Engleman. She directed an Ameliorative Preschool designed, as the title suggests, to ameliorate educational deficiencies. She achieved some success, but she is better known recently for a program of parent training called the Mothers' Training Program. In this program mothers were trained to tutor their own children. The projected outcome was to aid children with language development, increase intelligence, and help prepare children for school attitudinally.

Evaluations have shown children did improve in these areas. An interesting aspect of this study was a comparison of older siblings of the program children. The younger children showed more improvement, an indication that the mother's tutoring was effective (8, pp. 129-131).

Karnes's work reemphasizes the necessity of helping parents, as well as children, overcome cultural and educational deficits because much parental involvement and cooperation is needed in programs for young children.

White

Burton White at Harvard has been actively engaged in researching infant learning patterns for several years. He has also studied mothering techniques to determine what type of mother produces a more "competent" child. White believes that age three or four is too late to work with children to prevent academic difficulties in the future. In fact, he made the statement that programs designed to compensate for children's deficits, such as Head Start, are "not preventative, as advertised, but remedial."

The work of others could be cited, but we have summarized the theories of some of the best known researchers in areas relevant to early childhood education.

If there are some common threads running through the diverse body of research they would probably be:

1. The early years of life are of crucial importance to intellectual development.

2. Early intervention programs of many types appear to help make cognitive gains.

3. Parent and community concern and involvement are necessary to ensure success in early childhood programs.

In our next chapter we will examine some model programs that have resulted from this research and experimentation.

References

1. Bloom, Benjamin S. *Stability and Change in Human Characteristics.* New York: Wiley, 1964.

2. Hunt, J. McV. *Intelligence and Experience.* New York: Ronald Press, 1961.

3. Bruner, Jerome. *The Process of Education.* Cambridge, Mass.: Harvard University Press, 1960.

4. Evans, Ellis D. *Contemporary Influences in Early Childhood Education.* New York: Holt, Rinehart and Winston, Inc., 1971.

5. Willson, Victor L., et al. *Final Report Curriculum Revision Reports for St. Francis, Todd County and White River Schools.* ESEA Title I, University of South Dakota, 1976.

6. Deutsch, Martin, et al. *The Disadvantaged Child.* New York: Basic Books, 1967.

7. Deutsch, Martin, et al. *The Disadvantaged Child.* New York: Basic Books, 1967.

8. Hess, Robert D., and Croft, Doreen J. *Teachers of Young Children.* Boston, Mass.: Houghton Mifflin Co., 1975.

9. Weikart, David. *The Cognitively Oriented Curriculum: A Framework for Preschool Teachers.* Washington, D.C.: National Association for the Education of Young Children, 1971.

SUPPLEMENTAL REFERENCES

1. Bronfenbrenner, Urie. *Is Early Intervention Effective?* Washington, D.C.: Office of Child Development, U.S. Department of Health, Education and Welfare, 1974.

2. Becker, Wesley, and Engleman, Siegfried. *University of Illinois Follow-Through Approach: The Systematic Use of Reinforcement Principles.* Urbana, Illinois: University of Illinois Press, 1968.

3. Bereiter, Carl, and Engleman, Siegfried. *Teaching the Disadvantaged Child.* Englewood Cliffs, New Jersey: Prentice-Hall, 1966.

5. Karnes, Merle B. *Research and Development Program on Preschool Disadvantaged Children: Final Report.* Washington, D.C.: U.S. Office of Education, 1969.

6. Project Head Start. *Parent Involvement—A Workbook of Training Tips for Head Start Staff.* Washington, D.C.: Department of Health, Education and Welfare, 1968.

7. Spodek, Bernard. *Teaching in the Early Years.* Englewood Cliffs, New Jersey: Prentice-Hall, Inc., 1978.

Chapter 3
MODEL PROGRAMS

H ead Start and Follow Through programs have drawn extensively on the research and experimentation done in the area of early childhood education. Many of the early experimental programs of the sixties were refined and modified for both Head Start and Follow Through, and newer ones have been developed as well.

Some of the more prominent and successful experimental programs will be described in this chapter. It is well to remember that these model programs are more than materials. The curricular materials are certainly important, but the teaching approach and the philosophy underlying each program is equally important. Educators have not reached agreement on these varied approaches to early education, and some remain highly controversial. We can not discuss all the model programs, but a complete listing of them and their sponsors can be found at the end of this chapter. Further detailed information can be obtained directly from the individuals named.

Bank Street

A program of considerable merit which concentrated efforts on disadvantaged children was developed by the Bank Street College of Education in New York City. Here a stable, ordered environment, which frequently contrasts with disadvantaged children's chaotic home life, allows them to learn to trust and feel secure in a school situation. Cognitive language development follows this as a goal. The teacher plans and introduces activities, but teaching is done diagnostically, noting children's responses and weaknesses. A teacher follows through on each child's individual strengths and weaknesses. Academic skills are taught more incidentally than in some other programs, and the teacher's role is considered more important. Teaching must be consistent to attain a child's trust, since emotional development is a paramount goal.

A strong emphasis is placed on the development of a positive self-image. Since the program is rather individualized children have quite a bit of freedom to select activities they enjoy, but teachers also try to provide a balance of group activities (1, pp. 199-200).

This program supports strong parental involvement. This is generally true for all Head Start and Follow Through programs because the government requires that parents be actively involved in their children's education, although the application and extent of involvement may vary from program to program.

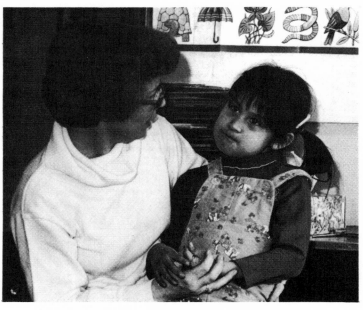

Bank Street stresses trust and positive self-image in the child.

Tucson Model

Another model program for Head Start and Follow Through is the Tucson Early Education Model developed at the University of Arizona. This program was originally developed for preschool and primary grade children who spoke Spanish as their primary language. The emphasis here is on much practical experience. Seeing, touching, doing, and simultaneously learning words to go with these experiences, help these children become functional in English as well as Spanish. The developers concentrated on four areas: language competence, intellectual base, motivational base, and societal arts and skills (1, pp. 194-195). All of the many projects in which the children engage are designed to promote these four main goals.

The program is now being used with children other than Mexican-Americans. The assumption underlying this broader application is that the lack of language skills has handicapped all disadvantaged children, not just those whose primary language is not English.

Open Education Model

Educational practices of the British Infant School model became increasingly popular throughout the United States in the early 1970s. The Infant School in England is for children ages five to seven, although there are nursery classes for three and four year olds in some British Infant Schools (2, pp. 27-55). This, of course, is the source for the much publicized "open classroom" movement. Learning centers, unstructured learning, and pursuit of individual, intellectual interests are some characteristics of these schools.

The specific model for Head Start and Follow Through has come from the Educational Development Center in Newton, Massachusetts. This plan is more of a teaching approach or philosophy than a programmatic model. EDC is more interested in creating classroom enviornments that are responsive to the needs and the interests of children than in specific materials or teaching style.

The British Infant School and the Head Start and Follow Through classrooms based on this British import concentrate on helping children become independent and self-motivated in a supportive atmosphere. The child's desire to learn is nurtured by building on individual interests and strengths. No specific materials are used, rather all kinds of books and supplies are provided. Creative activities are stressed. There are many more differences apparent and individual teacher's touches observable in the classrooms where this model is relied upon (3, pp. 51-61). For example, natural and home-made materials brought to school by children or teachers are thought to be as worthwhile as commercial materials. The sponsor provides lists of commercial materials which can be used, but this is a matter of choice for individual schools. The materials chosen reflect interests and curiosities of children.

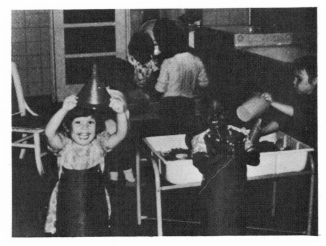

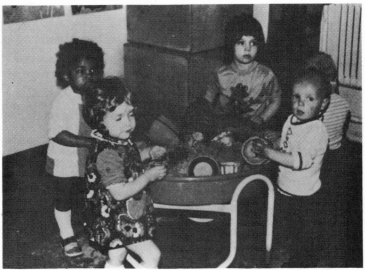

Children from the Nursery class in an Infant School in London enjoy sand and water centers

Engleman-Becker

Another model which contrasts sharply with some of the less structured programs is the Engleman-Becker Model, based on the experimentation and research done by Bereiter and Engleman which has already been discussed.

This program, DISTAR, has a complete set of materials for the areas of language, math, and reading. The children are taken through the materials in small, sequential steps. It is fast-moving, and children are tested frequently to analyze their progress. It is also a highly structured program in which the teacher does not deviate from the teacher's guide. There is a great deal of repetition and drill. Additional attention will be given the DISTAR materials in a later chapter, but the theory behind this approach is that disadvantaged children in Head Start and Follow Through must compensate quickly for their educational lacks in order to be competitive with other children later in their school experience (3, pp. 15-26).

The Cognitively Oriented Curriculum

This model is derived from Weikart's work in Ypsilanti, Michigan, and demands an orderly pattern of learning predicated on Piaget's developmental stages of childhood. We will look more closely at Piaget in the next chapter, but Weikart's curriculum for the young child emphasizes mastery of classification and seriation skills as well as emphasizing spatial and temporal relationships. This program requires rather sophisticated teachers who have been throughly trained in its effective implementation.

Briefly, it consists of logical development of the child's intelligence. First the child must reach the Object Level where he can identify and name objects. He then moves to the Index Level at which stage he can understand object permanence and relationships.

The next step is the Symbol Level. Here he can understand that pictures represent objects, then he reaches the Sign Level when he understands that printed words represent objects also (3, pp. 27-44).

Home visits to supplement and reinforce classroom learning are an integral part of this program.

The program emphasizes techniques used in highly structured programs like DISTAR, but also relies on some of the more open, learning-center methods of traditional nursery schools. However, everything is carefully coordinated and planned by the teacher to achieve the goal of improving cognitive abilities. Detailed, even intricate, plans are required of the teacher to ensure the success of this program. Results of some recent research conducted with Follow Through children indicate that third grade children in the program write more fluently, have better vocabularies, and are able to better organize their writing than non-Follow Through children (4, pp. 4-8).

DARCEE

This program grew out of the preschool early intervention studies done at Peabody College in the 1960s.

The program today is structured, but not rigidly. It is built around units or themes beginning with the child and expanding his horizons to include the family, neighborhood, and larger community. All these units are designed to improve the child's language skills. Activities vary from day to day, and large and small group activities are included.

DARCEE programs include a variety of curriculum materials, but the Peabody Language Development Kit and other Peabody materials are usually included. The kit contains a very complete teacher's manual, many pictures, and appealing puppets to aid in language teaching.

Home visits are also an important aspect of the program (3, pp. 68-82). This program is a Head Start, but not a Follow Through, model since it is confined to preschool children.

The Behavior Analysis Model

The Behavior Analysis Model, as the name implies, diagnoses individual children's weaknesses and helps them overcome them. This University of Kansas-based model relies heavily on behavior modification principles. Positive reinforcement in the form of tokens or chips are given frequently when children succeed. The tokens are exchanged for activities the child particularly enjoys, such as stories or games. Each child decides individually how to spend his earned tokens.

Basic skills such as reading and writing are emphasized, but attitudinal skills such as listening, following directions, and learning to cooperate are are also stressed as essential to later school achievement (3, pp. 45-50).

Appalachian Preschool Education Program

Federal funding of various regional laboratories throughout the nation has resulted in various programs. One of these is the Appalachian Preschool Education Program. In this program developed by the Appalachian Educational Laboratory, based in Charleston, West Virginia, a three-fold thrust is used. First the child is exposed to daily television lessons at home, which focus on language and reading. A definite reading vocabulary is introduced. Then, on a weekly basis, a trained teacher or paraprofessional visits the home to work with parents and child. This reinforces the television lesson and gets the parents actively involved in the child's educational program. The third part of the program allows the child to have the experience of working in a classroom situation in order to interact with other children and a teacher. A mobile classroom travels to where the children are, enabling a small group to meet on a once-a-week basis. Testing has indicated children involved in all three aspects of the program make the greatest gains (5). The television series associated with this program, "Around the Bend," has had enough success to prompt a second television effort. This will be a series of educational television programs for parents developed by the AEL.

Prentice-Hall Model

One other model which should be mentioned because of its uniqueness is the Prentice-Hall Follow Through Model. It is the only model presently being implemented that is sponsored by a commercial agency (Prentice-Hall, Inc. is a large publishing firm). This program appears only at one site, Kansas City, Missouri.

The program's individualized modes of instruction aid in the development of intellectual skills that will help children become successful members of society.

Some of the instructional materials are unusual, quite different from those in most other programs. They include the talking typewriter, a computerized typewriter, which gives the child audio and visual instruction and feedback. Another piece of equipment is the talking page. The child listens to recorded lessons in reading and math and completes the written work involved. The voice mirror is a third device used in the program. This is a type of tape recorder which provides immediate feedback without the necessity of rewinding the tape (6, pp. 193-206). The Prentice-Hall Field Math Laboratory, a set of manipulative materials, is used in math and science areas. Project staff are encouraged to develop and make additional materials to supplement the sponsor's curriculum. Varied learning centers that permit children to choose among alternatives are examples of staff input.

Home Start

Home Start began in 1972. It built on existing knowledge about the need for parents to become actively involved in children's education. Home Start was expected to provide the same comprehensive services that Head Start offers. Health, nutritional, and psychological help, as well as intellectual stimulation, were delivered. The principal difference between Head Start and Home Start was the emphasis on parents as teachers in the home environment; their involvement was the base of the entire effort. Assistance was offered parents so they could better teach their own children.

There were sixteen Home Start programs in the original federally funded study. These programs were scattered over the nation. They were both rural and urban and represented diverse cultural and ethnic groups. In 1976 the results of the four years' work were published and indicated that Home Start was an effective way to reach families and children. Parents showed a greater interest in all their children. The results also showed Home Start to be cost effective in relation to Head Start programs in the same communities.

A number of implications were also published in the same final report. Paraprofessional staff members can be effective providers of Home Start services; proper training and supervision of staff are necessary components of the program; specialists' help is also needed; evaluation needs to be ongoing.

There is no one typical Home Start program but behavioral goals in five areas are emphasized in all. They are termed "relationships" and include efforts to improve the following:

1. Relationship to self.

2. Children's relationships to adults and parents' relationships to children.

3. Relationships to peers.

4. Relationships to materials and ideas.

5. Relationship to a group. (7)

On the basis of its initial success Home Start will probably be continued along with Head Start and Follow Through.

Television Programs

One other very exciting program which is available to nearly all children, rural or urban, and which has had some interesting results is the television program "Sesame Street." It was planned originally by the Children's Television Workship, for disadvantaged city preschoolers. Its appeal has gone far beyond that, and it is even being shown in other countries. Plans are being carried out to broaden the scope of the original program. A newer thrust is "The Electric Company" designed for somewhat older children. Much research has been and is being based on television's impact on young children. School systems are frequently considering revision of their curriculum in view of the impact these television offerings have made.

The areas of agreement in all the foregoing programs are that early educational deficits can be overcome to some extent by early educational intervention, that very young children can learn much more than has been thought in the past, and that language development and other cognitive skills should be emphasized. There, however, agreement ends. Differences arise over how structured a learning situation should be for young children, about the relative stress that cognitive skills and affective skills should be given. Even motivational techniques differ, with some relying almost completely on tangible rewards and others trying to help children learn for the joy of learning.

It is probably important that teachers examine all these model programs and adopt an eclectic approach, selecting ideas and materials that will work in their particular situation.

A summary chart describing twenty Follow Through programs, sponsors, emphasis, and materials can be found on the following pages.

Follow Through Model Program Summary Chart

PROGRAM	SPONSOR	EMPHASIS	MATERIALS
Bank Street Model	Bank Street College of Education - New York City	Optimum human interaction and development	Trade books, Bank Street Readers, teacher-made, other
Interdependent Learning Model	City University of New York	Humanistic, interpersonal, noncompetitive intellectual growth	Many games, phonics-based reading, other basal readers
Home-School Partnership Model	Clark College - Atlanta, Georgia	Use of home environment, parents as teachers	Varied instructional materials, teacher-made materials
Responsive Education Program	Far West Laboratory for Educational Research and Development - San Francisco, California	Understanding cultural differences, problem solving, promoting good self-concept	Varied materials compatible with goals
Parent supported application of the Behavior Oriented Prescriptive Teaching Approach	Georgia State University - Atlanta, Georgia	Individual diagnoses and prescription for meaningful instruction	Teacher manuals, learning kits, games, other
Nongraded Follow Through Model	Hampton Institute - Hampton, Virginia	Nongraded, individualized continuous progress instruction	Varied materials, learning centers, teacher-made materials
Cognitively Oriented Curriculum Model	High/Scope Foundation - Ypsilanti, Michigan	Expansion of cognitive knowledge according to developmental abilities	Varied materials selected to fit the model

Program	Institution	Objectives	Materials
Cultural Linguistic Approach	Northeastern Illinois University - Chicago, Illinois	Acceptance of cultural patterns and linguistic skills and building upon them	...strategies, ethnic objects, Sullivan Reading Program
Follow Through Model	Prentice-Hall, Inc.	Attitudinal change through individualized academic growth	"Talking Typewriters", "Talking Page," "Voice Mirror," other materials
Language Development (Bilingual Education) Approach	Southwest Educational Development Laboratory - Austin, Texas	Instruction in Spanish or English, increasing self-esteem, oral language stress	Six instructional kits - multimedia
Tucson Early Education	University of Arizona - Tucson, Arizona	Stress on functional language competency, intellectual and social skills	Interest centers, varied materials, teacher-made kits
Culturally Democratic Learning Environments	University of California at Santa Cruz - Santa Cruz, California	Appreciation of cultural identity, promote intellectual flexibility	Varied materials, Spanish reading materials, cultural heritage units
Florida Parent Education Model	University of Florida - Gainesville, Florida	Home learning activities, parents as teachers	Home learning activities, varied instructional materials
Mathemagenic Activities Program	University of Georgia - Athens, Georgia	Knowledge acquired through interaction with total environment, developmental-intellectual growth	Instruction units, curriculum guides, workbooks, and other materials
Behavior Analysis Approach	University of Kansas - Lawrence, Kansas	Behavior analysis methods, positive reinforcement to promote academic progress	Model designed reading materials and other materials plus integration of other materials

MODEL PROGRAMS

Follow Through Model Program Summary Chart (continued)

PROGRAM	SPONSOR	EMPHASIS	MATERIALS
The New School Approach to Follow Through	University of North Dakota - Grand Forks, North Dakota	Encourage curiosity, inductive learning, self-direction	Learning centers, manuals, handbooks, varied other materials
Engleman-Becker Model for Direct Instruction	University of Oregon - Eugene, Oregon	Structured, programmed learning for optimum academic gains	DISTAR-reading, math and language materials
Individualized Early Learning Program	University of Pittsburgh - Pittsburgh, Pennsylvania	Individualized instruction for optimum mastery of cognitive material	PEP materials, learning centers, Sullivan Reading material, other materials
The Role-Trade Model	Western Behavioral Sciences Institute - La Jolla, California	Extension of classroom to home and neighborhood, understanding of varied roles in school, home, and community	Program produced materials, varied materials
EDC Open Education Model	Educational Development Center - Newton, Mass.	Stresses independent learning	Varied instruction materials, handbooks for teachers and parents

Listing of all Model Programs and addresses for obtaining further information:

1. The Bank Street Model
   Dr. Lorraine Smithberg
   Bank Street College of Education
   Follow Through Project
   610 West 112th Street
   New York, New York 10025

2. Interdependent Learning Model
   Mr. Harold Freeman, Jr.
   City University of New York
   Community Research and Service Center
   144 West 125th Street
   New York, New York 10027

3. Home-School Partnership Model
   Mrs. Johnnie R. Follins, Co-director
   Home-School Partnership Model
   Suite 200
   2945 Stone-Hogan Rd. Connector, SW
   Atlanta, Georgia 30331

   Mrs. Jean W. Humphrey, Co-director
   Home-School Partnership Model
   Suite 200
   2945 Stone-Hogan Rd. Connector, SW
   Atlanta, Georgia 30331

4. EDC Open Education Model
   Ms. Grace Hilliard, Director
   EDC Open Education Follow Through Project
   Education Development Center
   55 Chapel Street
   Newton, Massachusetts 02160

5. Responsive Education Model
   Dr. Denis Thoms
   Far West Laboratory for Educational Research and Development
   1855 Folsom Street
   San Francisco, California 94103

6. Behavior Oriented Prescriptive Teaching Model
   Dr. Walter Hodges
   Department of Early Childhood Education
   Georgia State University
   33 Gilmer Street, SE
   Atlanta, Georgia 30303

7. Nongraded Follow Through Model
   Dr. Mary T. Christian, Executive Director
   Nongraded Follow Through Model
   Department of Elementary Education
   Hampton Institute
   Hampton, Virginia 23668

8. The Cognitively Oriented Curriculum Model
   Dr. David P. Weikart
   High/Scope Cognitively Oriented Curriculum Model
   High/Scope Educational Research Foundation
   600 North River Street
   Ypsilanti, Michigan 48197

9. The Cultural Linguistic Approach
   Mr. Donald Linder
   Center for Inner City Studies
   4545 South Drexek Boulevard
   Chicago, Illinois 60653

10. Follow Through Model
    Ms. Marilyn Smetana
    Director of Follow Through Project
    Prentice-Hall Developmental Learning Centers, Inc.
    P.O. Box 293
    West Orange, New Jersey 07051

11. Language Development (Bilingual Education) Model
    Dr. Preston C. Kronosky
    Director, Follow Through Division
    Southwest Educational Development Laboratory
    211 East Seventh Street
    Austin, Texas 78701

12. Tucson Early Education Model
    Joseph M. Fillerup, Director
    TEEM Follow Through Program
    Arizona Center for Educational Research and Development
    College of Education - 439
    University of Arizona
    Tucson, Arizona 85721

13. Culturally Democratic Learning Environments
    Dr. Manuel Ramirez, III
    Follow Through Director
    University of California, Santa Cruz
    25 Social Science Building
    Santa Cruz, California 95064

14. Florida Parent Education Model
    Dr. Gordon E. Greenwood, Co-director
    University of Florida
    520 Weil Hall
    Gainesville, Florida 32611

15. Mathemagenic Activities Model
    Dr. Charles D. Smock
    Mathemagenic Activities Program
    Psychology Building, Room 229
    University of Georgia
    Athens, Georgia 30602

16. Behavior Analysis Model
    Dr. Eugene Ramp
    University of Kansas
    Support and Development Center for Follow Through
    Department of Human Development
    Lawrence, Kansas 66045

17. The New School Approach to Follow Through
    Dr. Vito Perrone
    The New School Approach to Follow Through
    Center for Teaching and Learning
    University of North Dakota
    Grand Forks, North Dakota 58201

18. Engelman-Becker Model for Direct Instruction
    Siegfried Engelman and Wesley C. Becker, Co-directors
    University of Oregon Follow Through Project
    Department of Special Education
    Eugene, Oregon 97403

19. The Individualized Early Learning Model
    Dr. R. Tony Eichelberger, Co-principal Investigator
    Ms. M. Elizabeth Boston, Co-principal Investigator
    Follow Through Project
    Learning Research and Development Center
    3939 O'Hara Street
    Pittsburgh, Pennsylvania 15260

    Dr. Lauren Resnick
    Dr. Warren Shepler
    Follow Through Project
    Learning Research and Development Center
    3939 O'Hara Street
    Pittsburgh, Pennsylvania 15260

20. The Role-Trade Model
    Dr. Wayman J. Crow
    Western Behavioral Sciences Institute
    1150 Silverado Street
    La Jolla, California 92037

Preschool Only—Not Follow Through Models

The DARCEE Model
Susan Gray
George Peabody College for Teachers
Nashville, Tennessee 37203

Appalachia Educational Laboratory
P.O. Box 1348
Charleston, West Virginia 25325

References

1. Hess, Robert D., and Croft, Doreen J. *Teachers of Young Children.* Boston, Mass: Houghton-Mifflin Co. 1972.

2. *Primary Education.* London, England: Her Majesty's Stationery Office, 1959.

3. Chow, Stanley H.L., and Elmore, Patricia. *Early Childhood Information Unit, Resource Manual and Program Descriptions.* Educational Products Information Exchange (EPIE) Institute, 1973.

4. "Research Report: The Productive Language Assessment Tasks." *Bulletin of the High/Scope Foundation,* no. 3 Winter 1976.

5. *Model Programs, Childhood Education, Appalachia Preschool Education Program.* Washington, D.C.: U.S. Government Printing Office, 1970.

6. *Follow Through, A Resource Guide to Sponsor Modes and Materials.* Washington, D.C.: Office of Education, HEW, 1976.

7. Nevius, John R. and Filgo, Dorothy J. *Home Start Education: A Guideline to Content Areas.* Washington, D.C.: Office of Child Development, HEW, 1976.

SUPPLEMENTARY REFERENCES

1. Athey, I.J., and Rubadeau, N.J. *Educational Implications of Piaget's Theory: A Book of Readings.* Waltham, Mass.: Blaisdell Publishing Co., 1971.

2. Bereiter, C. *Acceleration of Intellectual Development in Early Childhood.* Urbana, Illinois: University of Illinois, 1967.

3. Blackie, J. *Inside the Primary School.* London, England: Her Majesty's Stationary Office, 1967

4. Deutsch, M. *The Disadvantaged Child.* N.Y.: Basic Books, 1967.

5. Featherstone, J. *Schools Where Children Learn.* N.Y.: Liveright, 1961.

6. Pines, Maya.   Revolution in Learning: The Years From Birth to Six.   N.Y.: Harper and Row, 1967.

7. U.S. Office of Education. *It Works: Preschool Program in Compensatory Education.* Washington, D.C.: Government Printing Office, 1968.

8. Weber, L.   *The English Infant School and Informal Education.*   Worthington, Ohio: Charles A. Jones Publishing Co., 1970.

9. Weikart, D. *The Cognitively Oriented Curriculum: A Framework for Preschool Teachers.* Washington, DC: National Association for the Education of Young Children, 1971.

Chapter 4

CHILD DEVELOPMENT THEORIES

A number of scholars have evolved theories about the developmental stages of children. But how can we determine which is the best or the right theory? Perhaps all we can do here is look at the work of these various thinkers and attempt a synthesis that will prove useful.

Freud

Although Freud's work was done many years ago, numerous people still subscribe to his ideas. Others, called neo-Freudians, adhere to a modified interpretation of Freud. At any rate, Freud's developmental stages of childhood still hold enough interest to warrant his inclusion. Freud saw human beings as sexual beings from birth on and was inclined to attach sexual, or perhaps sensual, connotations to much human behavior. Freud's construct of human behavior is quite complicated and involved, but for our purposes, let's simply say that Freud saw the child going through a series of psychosexual developmental stages paralleling the cognitive emergence of the ego and identified various adult personality traits as direct outcomes of experiences in these various childhood periods. The first of these is the oral stage. This generally lasts through the first year and a half or longer. Young infants receive primary satisfaction orally; and because it is pleasurable to receive nourishment, they find other oral activities satisfying. They try everything in their mouth. Sucking provides comfort and pleasure even without getting food. Thumb sucking often starts; and if infants do not receive sufficient oral satisfaction, they may become fixated and seek oral stimulation and gratification long past the usual oral period. It naturally follows that adult behavior such as compulsive eating, or smoking a pipe, or other means of seeking gratification orally is seen as going back to infancy and a lack of sufficient gratification in the oral period of life.

The next stage the very young child moves into is the anal period. It is assumed that the child enjoys stimulation of this part of the body. Freud thought this refocusing of attention from the oral to the anal area of the body was simply a part of natural development or that it was maturational. Others succeeding Freud attribute this period to the attention given this area of the body during the toilet training process. At any rate, there is some agreement that toilet training and the manner in which it is handled may have great effect on an individual's personality in maturity. A child really has the upper hand in the toilet training process, and undue stress can cause a child to withhold bowel movements or conversely to present them to receive his parent's praise. The characteristic of retentiveness is thought to be a fixation of the anal period, and some people fixated in the period indicate excessive concern with holding onto money or possessions or even people—the overly possessive mother, for example. Another aspect of this period is a concern with cleanliness, simple enough to understand in the toilet training period itself, but fraught with long-range implications. The person fixated in this stage may be unduly fussy and neat, desirous of orderliness, both mental and physical.

By the age of four the child has usually passed through this stage and has entered the phallic stage, when the interest and pleasure feelings are focused on the genital region. This is further complicated in psychoanalytic theory by the Oedipus complex. Again, resolution of sexual problems of this age are necessary for normal development, or later complications occur.

Finally, at about age six the child's sexual feelings are thought to subside, and the child enters a latency period, which lasts roughly through the early elementary years of school until the beginning of adolescence. This is considered a stable quiescent time when sex feelings may not actually recede, but children are so busy acquiring culture and learning their role in society that sexual feelings do not dominate (1, pp. 305-374).

You can see how important the early childhood years are in the Freudian outlook. By the time the children are seven or eight they have gone through three major Freudian stages and part of a fourth.

Erikson

A more recent theorist is Erik Erikson. Erikson leaned heavily on Freud, but where Freud described his psychosexual stages, Erikson's developmental stages are called psychosocial and these stages relate to personality growth.

In fact, a simple way to keep in mind three major theorists discussed in this chapter is to refer to the following table.

THEORIST	TYPE OF DEVELOPMENTAL STAGES
Freud	Psychosexual stages
Erikson	Psychosocial stages
Piaget	Stages of intellectual development

The first four of Erikson's stages are indicated below. These are the stages with which those in early childhood education are most concerned although the reader must be aware that the stages continue through adolescence to adulthood.

1. *Basic trust versus basic mistrust.* Similar to Freud's oral stage, the development of a sense of trust dominates the first year. Success means coming to trust the world, other people, and himself. Since the mouth is the main zone of pleasure, trust grows on being fed when hungry, pleasant sensations when nursing, and the growing conviction that his own actions have something to do with pleasant events. Consistent, loving care is trust-promoting. Mistrust develops when trust-promoting experiences are inadequate, when the baby has to wait too long for comfort, when he is handled harshly or capriciously. Since life is never perfect, shreds of mistrust are woven into the fabric of personality. Problems of mistrust recur and have to be solved later, but when trust is dominant, healthy personality growth takes place.

2. *Autonomy versus shame and doubt.* The second stage, corresponding to Freud's anal period, predominates during the second and third year. Holding on and letting go with the sphincter muscles symbolizes the whole problem of autonomy. The child wants to do for himself with all of his powers: his new motor skills of walking, climbing, manipulating; his mental powers of choosing and deciding. If his parents give him plenty of suitable choices, times to decide when his judgment is adequate for successful outcomes, then he grows in autonomy. He gets the feeling that he can control his body, himself, and his environment. The negative feelings of doubt and shame arise when his choices are disastrous, when other people shame him or force him in areas where he could be in charge.

3. *Initiative versus guilt.* The Oedipal part of genital stage of Freudian theory, 4 and 5 years, is to Erikson the stage of development of a sense of initiative. Now the child explores the physical world with his senses and the social and physical worlds with his questions, reasoning, imaginative, and creative powers. Love relationships with parents are very important. Conscience develops. Guilt is the opposite pole of initiative.

4. *Industry versus inferiority.* Solutions of problems of initiative and guilt bring about entrance to the stage of developing a sense of industry, the latency period of Freud. The child is now ready to be a worker and producer. He wants to do jobs well instead of merely starting them and exploring them. He practices and learns the rules. Feelings of inferiority and inadequacy result when he feels he cannot measure up to the standards held for him by his family or society (2, p. 279).

Gesell

Another theorist who should be considered is Arnold Gesell. His work was done at Yale University primarily during the 1920s and 30s. He and his colleagues studied thousands of children to observe all facets of child behavior. Their observations were carefully recorded, some on film, for future study and analysis. After a great deal of data had been gathered, Gesell felt "norms" could be established, and he could make generalizations about child behavior at various ages.

Based on this work Gesell presented a theory which has become known as the maturational-developmental theory. In this theory all development depends on natural maturation, and all children will progress through the various ages and stages in much the same manner. Gesell did believe in developmental stages, but thought that nearly all normal, healthy children display the same behavior at about the same age period. Educators seemed to subscribe to this theory for a long time and developed curriculum material under the assumption that all children could read at nearly the same level at the same age. All second graders were expected to learn to subtract and all fourth graders were expected to learn to multiply. This has not proved to be true in actual practice, however.

Gesell's work has been of great value to those interested in child development and much of his normative data are still studied but Gesell has been criticized in recent times for his failure to consider the child's environment and its effect on development. Educators today believe extrinsic factors, as well as heredity and biology, play a part in the child's development. It must be understood, however, that Gesell and his coworkers did not take an extreme position in their maturational theory. They only offered approximate norms with scope for individual variations. Gesell has also been criticized for studying primarily middle and upper middle-class children rather than including all classes and cultural groups in his sample.

However, in all fairness, the Gesell Institute of Child Development produced vast quantities of materials which are still relied upon, in spite of recent questions about the validity of the maturational theory. Numerous books, articles, maturity tests, and other publications grew out of the work of the institute. The book *The First Five Years of Life* (3) delineates detailed behavior patterns that can be expected of the child in the first five years of life. This book has probably been one of the most valuable resources for those concerned with young children.

Piaget

Of the other theoretical people in this field, perhaps the most important name, and the one having the greatest impact today, is Jean Piaget. Piaget published books on his theories as far back as the 1920s but his work has only attracted widespread attention in recent years. Piaget, who is Swiss and still active in Geneva, Switzerland, has written voluminously. He started his professional career as a biologist, and this orientation is often evident in his terminology.

The child's development is divided into four main periods in Piaget's theory. The first one is the sensorimotor period which extends from birth to two years. This is, of course, the age we think of as infancy, and the child makes tremendous strides here. He goes from purely motor activity to some mental activity. Gradually the child is able to look at things outside himself. External objects are explored, and in the final stages of this period he is able to engage in goal oriented activities. He is still "perception bound," but from purely physical activity he has developed some understandings and comprehends in a limited way such things as causality, space, the reality of objects, and, often, their functions. He is learning rapidly through imitation. You have certainly seen a young child trying to copy many adult activities. He can come up with reasons or explanations which are not necessarily accurate, but that satisfy him.

Next the child moves into the period of preoperational thought which lasts from about two to seven years. The child's intellectual structure evolves during this period. Several outstanding characteristics mark this stage. The child is egocentric; he cannot be reasoned with in a logical manner; and contradictions don't disturb him. He sees everything in terms of himself and his personal environment. His ideas are concrete, and he does not think in abstractions. There must be a concrete explanation for everything that happens even if it requires attributing life and thought to inanimate objects. This animistic approach seems a necessary part of children's mental apparatus at this time because it enables them to explain otherwise unexplainable phenomena.

Some of the unique features of Piaget's view of this period of life involve a knowledge of his terminology. He deals with the term "conservation" at length and his understanding of conservation is permanency of mass, weight, and volume in substances. The child cannot see that something could differ in appearance but remain the same in volume, weight, etc. The classic example in Piaget's experiments with children involves pouring milk from a low, wide glass into a tall, narrow glass. The child will usually say there is more milk in the tall glass. He is unable to perceive in the first part of this stage that the two glasses could both hold the same amount of milk. In another example a lump of clay may be stretched out until it is quite different in appearance from the original lump. The child will often say the new clay shape is bigger and heavier than it was in the beginning. Piaget's studies show that children master the concepts of conservation sequentially. The understanding of conservation of mass comes about age seven; the understanding of conservation of weight and volume doesn't emerge until a few years later.

A Piagetian curriculum would feature such developmental tasks as seriation or sequencing of pictures.

So, although the child makes vast gains in learning, he is not ready to deal with abstract problems concerning numbers, quantity, movement, and other related areas. In other words, although the child is certainly thinking, and has advanced from the sensorimotor period, the thought is still preoperational. Naturally, the next step is into the period of concrete operations, lasting from seven to eleven years. This stage and the final one, formal operations, will not be discussed here since they are not germane to our study.

Piaget's theories provide an understanding of how children learn and what they can learn in a particular stage, which is of great value in developing programs and curriculum for the young child, and, in fact, for the older child as well. The implications for teaching very young children are important. Some preschool programs, such as the cognitively oriented curriculum mentioned previously, are actually based on Piaget's findings.

Newly developed curriculum materials have relied on Piaget's work, and we shall probably continue to see it as a potent force in all levels of education.

Bruner

Still others are working on theories of child development and learning. A consideration of Bruner logically follows Piaget since much of his work has been based on Piaget's. He has attempted to clarify and modify Piaget's work to some extent and his vocabulary is somewhat different from Piaget's. Bruner has already been mentioned in connection with current research and experiments. Of course, we are dealing primarily with the cognitive or intellectual sphere of development when we speak of the work of these two men. Bruner's findings are quite similar to Piaget's. He shows that the ways that children behave and learn are sequential. They must first see and manipulate real objects. This is "enactive" representation. Later they can recall the object mentally without seeing or touching, and this is called the "iconic" level; still later they can put a name to a mental image and they have then reached the "symbolic" level. Part of Bruner's work, which may well prove to be the most important part, is an attempt to discover how teaching will affect the change from the iconic to symbolic level. In other words, does instruction affect language growth and progress? Bruner feels symbolic ability is more than just a maturational fact, and children could learn more at earlier ages if proper instruction was given (4).

Skinner

B.F. Skinner is a psychologist who has had a profound effect on the field of psychology and on education. Skinner has not put forth a developmental theory like those we have been considering, but he has produced a learning theory that has provided a theoretical basis for numerous programs and materials used in early childhood education and, in fact, at all levels of education. Skinner's work at Harvard has made him the foremost proponent of behavioristic psychology today.

Skinner and his colleagues have reached the conclusion that humans are governed by external stimuli and that, by controlling the stimuli received, human behavior can be controlled. Human behavior can be modified if a knowledgeable person manipulates the stimuli. Human actions can be quite predictable and behavior can be changed. "Behavior mod," a shortened form of the term "behavior modification," is a common way of referring to such behavior control.

The work of earlier behaviorists has been built upon by Skinner. One of the earliest classic examples of "conditioning," or behavior control, was Pavlov and his famous dogs. The dogs learned to associate food with sounds and then began salivating reflexively with only the sound. Interestingly, after a period when the dogs received no food following the sound, the salivating behavior was extinguished. Others, such as Thorndike and Watson, did further work in this area, so Skinner commenced his research with a solid background on which to build.

Skinner worked a long time with animals, conditioning them to respond to different stimuli when their behavior was rewarded, or reinforced. For instance, rats and pigeons learned to push levers to obtain food. Then Skinner tried to extract his findings and adapt them to human behavior. In his view human learning is conditioning and not dissimilar to the animals' learning to push a button and get a reward of food.

His term "operant conditioning" means the learner's response is stimulated by a certain stimulus, and if it is a response that is rewarded or reinforced the learned behavior will continue. An example of this would be:

> An infant accidentally touches an object near him in his crib and a tinkling bell-sound comes forth. The infant may look toward the source of the sound momentarily. Later, by chance perhaps, he again brushes his hand against the toy and the bell tinkles. In time we observe that he touches the toy with increasing frequency and looks at it. In this simple example we see illustrated the process of operant conditioning. . .which Skinner calls reinforcement. It is through this conditioning process we refer to as learning that Skinner believes most behavior is acquired (5, p. 49).

This theory of learning is much more complex than this brief explanation would indicate but it does have important implications for education. Skinner says teachers can expedite learning by controlling the stimuli and providing appropriate reinforcement. To do this the teaching material should be presented in small, carefully sequenced steps with frequent reinforcement. A further quotation may serve to explain this further.

> First of all, Skinner asks, what reinforcements are available for teachers? The material to be learned can itself have considerable automatic reinforcement. Knowing this, most teachers plan ways to make school work interesting. Furthermore, there are many things in a classroom that have appeal for students, such as toys, paints, scissors and paper, puzzles, library books, musical recordings. Often these sustain activity and may be used effectively by teachers as reinforcers for appropriate behavior. The net amount of reinforcement, Skinner points out, is of little significance. Very slight reinforcement can be very effective if appropriately used.
>
> If natural reinforcers inherent in the subject matter or in the school are not enough, contrived reinforcements must be used to control behavior. . . .
>
> Another question is how are reinforcements to be made contingent on the appropriate behavior? Skinner's answer is that becoming competent in any subject matter area is accomplished by dividing the material into very small steps. Reinforcement must be contingent upon the completion of each step satisfactorily. By making each successive step in the schedule as small as possible, reinforcements will occur frequently (5, pp. 74-75).

It is not difficult to see how this learning theory leads to "programmed" learning materials. The impact of Skinnerian behaviorism, while controversial, has nonetheless been felt throughout the educational world, but perhaps nowhere more strongly than in early childhood education.

Montessori

Before leaving the theorists we must discuss Maria Montessori. She was more of a practitioner than a theorist, yet she did some important and far-reaching work on theory, too. Montessori was a fascinating person and a pioneer in many ways. She was the first woman physician in Italy. She was able to accomplish amazing results working with indigent Italian children, who were considered hopelessly educationally retarded. She saw nursery education as essential and worked out a specific program designed to develop initiative and the child's perceptual abilities. Montessori, as with the other theorists, also adhered to the concept of sequential stages of cognitive development. She termed these stages of learning "sensitive periods." In Montessori's theoretical construct of human mental development age periods overlap considerably, but in a general way she saw the very young child as an "absorbent mind" ready first for sensory experiences, then language development. At the same time, muscle development and coordination were occurring. If the child did not have the opportunity to develop during the sensitive times when he was ready for these sequential learnings, he would be seriously handicapped later.

As children mature, they refine their physical movements further and become ever more curious intellectually. By age four a child is concerned with truth, reality, and temporal and spatial order. During the period from three to six most children can develop their tactile senses fully along with writing and reading skills. This assumes that children wish to learn, and, under sympathetic, encouraging environmental conditions, that they are continuously educating themselves.

The Montessori schools had, and still have, a rather highly structured approach. Every child goes through the material at his own pace step by step with the emphasis on learning to discover for himself. "Learning to learn" is the primary goal. Ideally the children can proceed independently and can even learn to read without help by first learning to write. They have sufficient self-discipline to continue on their own. Independence is a goal. Children must take care of themselves with little or no help in a Montessori school. It is not the teacher's responsibility to help with difficult boots or ties and zippers; it is the child's responsibility. Great emphasis is put on concrete tactile experiences. There are many materials to be manipulated. In light of all the research and the theories advanced today, it is clear that Montessori was far ahead of her time when she started her schools early in the twentieth century. Montessori schools do a lot of work with language, even introducing a foreign language to young children. This is just a further extension of Montessori's philosophy that children can learn to learn. French language instruction may often be a part of Montessori programs, with young children's proven ability in language mastery capitalized upon. (6, pp. 29-90). Montessori schools still use a great variety of material designed to help children in "auto-learning." Many of these toys or learning games were originally developed by Dr. Montessori herself and are seen by many as one of the strongest components of Montessori schools today.

Summary

How could all this information be summed up in order to apply it in a practical way in an early childhood classroom? We need to remember that the preschool years are ones of great development; the child is ready to explore the environment and discover much in his quest for knowledge. All children go through sequential stages in the development of the intellect. Children can absorb a tremendous amount of language learning, but we must also remember there are limitations. They are discovering themselves and their identity. There may be emotional problems which handicap the total development since they are extremely egocentric. A positive self-concept must be fostered. We must remember Piaget's work, which tells us the child cannot work well with abstractions. Children need concrete, repetitive experiences, and they learn a great deal by imitation. They need good adult models as well as the opportunity to interact with other children. These statements should apply regardless of the theory of development to which you subscribe.

The next chapter will probe the sociological aspects of early childhood education.

References

1. Baldwin, A.L. *Theories of Child Development.* New York: John Wiley and Sons, 1968.

2. Smart, Mollie S. and Russell C. *School Age Children.* New York: Macmillan, Inc., 1973.

3. Gesell, Arnold, et al. *The First Five Years of Life.* New York: Harper and Row, 1940.

4. Bruner, J.S., et al. *Studies in Cognitive Growth.* New York: John Wiley and Sons, 1966.

5. Molhollan, Frank and Forisha, Bill E. *From Skinner to Rogers.* Lincoln, Nebraska: Professional Educators Publications, Inc., 1972.

6. Lellard, Paula P. *Montessori, a Modern Approach.* New York: Schocken Books, 1972.

SUPPLEMENTARY REFERENCES

1. Flavel, J. *The Developmental Psychology of Jean Piaget.* Princeton, New Jersey: Van Nostrand Co., 1963.

2. Evans, Ellis D. *Contemporary Influences in Early Childhood Education.* New York: Holt, Rinehart and Winston, Inc., 1971.

3. Fisher, Dorothy C. *The Montessori Manual for Teachers and Parents.* Boston: Robert C. Bentley, Inc., 1964.

4. Frost, Joe L. *Early Childhood Education Rediscovered.* New York: Holt, Rinehart and Winston, Inc., 1968.

5. Montessori, Maria. *The Absorbent Mind.* New York: Dell, 1967.

6. Piaget, Jean. *The Origins of Intelligence in Children.* New York: W.W. Norton, 1963.

7. Standing, E. M. *Maria Montessori: Her Life and Work.* New York: New American Library, 1962.

Chapter 5

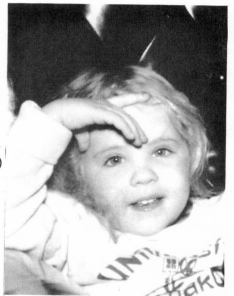

SOCIOLOGICAL
ASPECTS
OF EARLY
CHILDHOOD
EDUCATION

We have considered a variety of theories and programs. It is now necessary to examine the education of the very young child as it fits into the whole social scene. What sort of social trends affect the child's early education and development?

American Society Today

First we should take a look at the national social picture since, in a generalized way, social and technological factors have an important effect on us all. The American life style is constantly evolving. The mass media, particularly television, have changed life for everyone, and the effects of automation, shorter work week, and other technological changes have also been felt by all. Computers, for example, have changed our living patterns in many ways. The danger of nuclear weapons hovers over the world. Concern with pollution and maintenance of an ecological balance is part of life today. Social movements such as the civil rights movement, school desegregation, feminism, and efforts to eradicate poverty have affected the whole society to a great degree.

Small children are particularly susceptible to all the social forces which affect the family. The ever increasing divorce rate, the apparent weakening of the family structure, as well as the high mobility of people today are factors which obviously affect young children very greatly. The existing separation of Americans by social class, sex, economic status, and ethnic or racial factors has important end results for young children and for early childhood education. But, perhaps the societal change having the greatest impact on young children is the greatly increased number of women in the labor force today.

United States Census information reveals that in 1973 both the mother and father worked in over twenty million families. In that same year there were over thirty million working women with children (1). In 1976 there were more than sixteen million female heads of families; many of these women provided the sole support of their children. Six million working mothers have preschool children at home (2, p. 38). More than one-half of all young black children live in single parent homes and more than one-fourth of America's white school children live in broken families (3).

The need for quality day care programs becomes more obvious when statistics like these are made known. For these six million working mothers there are only one million day care openings. The less affluent members of our society are those most likely to have makeshift, inadequate child care arrangements.

In spite of the limited provisions that have been made for child care, many sociologists and economists indicate that if all married women were to stop working the results would be economically catastrophic for most families and the economic well-being of the nation. Wives' and mothers' incomes are essential, and women often have no choice about working (4, p. 14).

Since this situation will in all probability continue, the nation needs to show more concern, first, for providing sufficient child care, and, second, for upgrading the quality of day care to include high quality educational experiences rather than just custodial care. With all that is presently known about the great importance of the child's formative years from birth to age eight it is amazing that the United States should be so shortsighted about its children's well-being and future academic and social development.

Other Western industrialized nations have done much better by their children. Denmark is a good example. While the Danes believe firmly in "letting children be children," and nothing that could be termed formal education is begun until age seven, anyone who has visited and studied there can have no doubt about the Danish concern for children. There is a remarkable blending of day care, kindergarten, and playground facilities in

Denmark. Kindergarten is an informal experience not connected in any way with later public schooling.

When new housing is built to replace substandard living units an effort is always made to provide for the needs of all ages. Large, well-staffed playgrounds are included. Day care centers and kindergartens are an integral part of such new communities, as are club buildings for school age children where many kinds of interests from crafts to cooking can be pursued (5).

Sweden is another nation which shows great regard for the care and adequate development of children with working mothers. Olaf Palme, who was prime minister of Sweden for many years, conveys the Swedish attitude best in his own words:

> The most important form of service is the nursery school, where the children can be while their parents are working. We therefore plan strong expansion of nursery schools. The goal is that all children will be able to go. Some of the children may stay for only three hours, others for a longer period, depending on whether the parents work, study or prefer to be at home. We have become more conscious of how important the first few years of the children's lives are for their emotional and intellectual development later in life. The nursery school can compensate those children who do not get as much cultural stimulus at home as they should have.
>
> We should also like working hours to be shorter for parents with , small children. We are now heading for a general reduction of working hours. The forty-hour week will soon be carried into effect generally, and developments point to a further reduction. If the reduction in working hours is in the form of shorter daily working hours and not a prolonged vacation over the weekends it will be easier for both men and women to combine work with the role of parents (4, p. 256).

With such goals as Palme describes above, Sweden has done a superior job of meeting the needs of young children and their parents. The government, both national and local, plays a major role in regulating, operating, and subsidizing extensive day nursery programs.

Inequities In Society And Education

The social system in the United States has shown glaring deficiencies and inequities. We can elaborate a little further on this theme.

You will recall that most early childhood education programs for disadvantaged children have greatly emphasized language development. Language usage tends to reflect very noticeable class differences. Middle-class children are likely to be highly verbal. They speak in sentences, and have vocabularies that enable them to think consciously. Disadvantaged children have much more limited vocabularies. They often do not speak in sentences. Some large minority groups don't speak English at all. That there are very large class-linked language differences is indisputable.

The reasons are many. Children from the restricted environment of the urban ghetto have less opportunity to acquire language skill, or at least skill in standard English, as read and spoken by the middle-class American. Their experiences are severely limited in contrast with their more advantaged contemporaries. Language needs to serve a useful purpose to be functional, and for the middle-class child it is. For disadvantaged children, this is not so true; or perhaps we can say their language is functional, but in a much more limited way. They lack referents for a great many words that are easily understood by the middle-class child. Evidence supports the idea that disadvantaged children's thinking processes may be impaired, or at least much less developed, because they lack the words to think in a complex manner. Martin Deutsch indicates that cultural deprivation results in poor or limited sense perception (6, pp. 67-8). That is sight, hearing, and perhaps even touch may be less stimulated and thus less developed.

Class differences still appear to be enormous. The polarization of our society about which we hear and read so much may begin in the preschool years. The gulf that separates disadvantaged children in our society from their more advantaged counterparts looms larger and becomes increasingly formidable as children grow older. This is particularly true in language development and is the reason for the frantic effort to compensate in these early years.

We have considered adequate socialization of the young as a major purpose of early childhood education. How can this be accomplished successfully with the widely disparate backgrounds represented by young children? This is a very difficult problem which has not been adequately solved. There is a desire to retain cultural pluralism that continually conflicts with striving for some degree of standardization in our educational practices.

There is great variety in child rearing practices in our country, and unquestionably some of these practices are not conducive to success in the school setting dominated by a white Anglo-Saxon Protestant culture. Many disadvantaged children have been conditioned before they ever enter a public school classroom to be apathetic, or negative and hostile. These children will soon be defeated. They expect to be losers and they are. If the child's family and cultural background has prepared him to be passive, quiet, and not to call attention to himself the chances are he will not do well in a competitive classroom situation. Some minority groups, for example some Indian tribes, encourage this sort of behavior. However, inadequate socialization of young children is not restricted to any one group. Many children from a variety of backgrounds enter our schools with similar problems. Again the way of life in the home may be largely responsible. Two parents, or even one, in many cases, may fail to provide all the training into the ways of living that the extended family could provide. Making socialization the complete responsibility of one or two adults can result in children who don't become adequately socialized. This is called by some sociologists "dysfuntional socialization." Such a child could enter school with some serious lacks.

In order to overcome child-rearing deficiencies, the entire community must assume the responsibility for the education and welfare of its children. However, this is not presently being done to a great degree as indicated in the following quotation:

> One assumption in the educative community is that one of the main purposes of the school is to serve all people in a variety of ways, and, by so doing, schools will also serve the larger society. However, the many current problems in our society are at least partial evidence that the school is not serving all people. The schools have not been very successful in involving parents in planning for education, in relating curriculum to family problems and in developing problem-solving ability that can be used throughout a lifetime.
>
> For example, when teachers present only subject-centered information and assume that the health and welfare of the child should be taken care of elsewhere, their very effectiveness as subject matter specialists can be lessened. The education of the child is influenced by the total environment in which he or she exists, including the home, the neighborhood, and the school. What is taught and how it is taught needs to be made relevant to everyday life.
>
> Who, then, is involved in the educational process? In any community there are four main contributors: (1) the parents, (2) the community, (3) the child's peers, and (4) the schoolteacher. The purpose of the school in the educative community is to promote positive contributions by each (7, p. 57).

In addition to lack of community support there are further problems. There are also variations in the social role children perceive for themselves according to their race, sex, or subculture. Some studies show that black children think of themselves as inferior to whites. They ascribe a less important social role to their own race (8, pp. 63, 64). Other subculture affiliations can have a profound effect on the young child, such as some religious groups that prepare children to live quite differently from the majority in our present day society; the Hutterites in the upper Midwest and Canada are one example.

We must always be aware that each child has been exposed to different lifestyles and patterns of behavior. Such cultural variations mean many different ideas, attitudes, and values are present. The interaction among young children is a vital part of their development, and the teacher, especially, has a great responsibility to socialize the child.

Teachers Of Young Children

Is the allegation true that nearly all teachers are middle class themselves? If so, how can they cope with the variety of children, and particularly with the culturally deprived, present in many schools?

It is true that many teachers are middle class, although the number is decreasing. Often teaching has attracted socially mobile people from the working class or lower middle class who hope to move up the social ladder. Regardless of origins, most teachers are middle class by virtue of their life style, education, value system, and aspirations. This has been seen by many sociologists and educators as a severe problem. The needs of disadvantaged children simply have not been met in the past by such teachers. Teachers were inclined to expect recognition and understanding of their standards and value systems, which simply couldn't exist for these children. Such children were often labeled as mentally deficient or just incapable of learning. However, recognition of this problem has brought about some improvement. In fact, much of what we have previously mentioned about recent developments in early childhood education has been developed because this problem has been identified. The result is that continuing efforts are being made to provide a meaningful, effective educational program for all children in our society, regardless of class or ethnic identity.

Teacher Education

Are there teacher education programs that equip middle-class teachers to teach all kinds of children in early childhood programs, and do it well? Can teachers receive an excellent education that prepares them to teach in the area of early childhood?

Many colleges and universities are not providing specific training in this field—a real lack in teacher education institutions. The preparation of teachers has often not kept pace with the dynamic growth of early childhood education.

Until the last few years the preparation of teachers has been limited, and if any specialized training was provided it was often restricted to one course in kindergarten education. This is hardly sufficient. The graduate picture was even more bleak. This, however, is changing rapidly. Some of the same colleges and universities which five years ago lacked a sufficient program are developing programs that enable teachers to specialize in teaching the very young child. Since it is now possible to receive good preparation for early childhood education it would certainly be wise for parents to inquire into the educational background of any teacher to whom they entrust their child.

Educational qualifications are inextricably tied in with the role expectations of teachers. For instance, the ideal teacher of very young children understands children's social, emotional, intellectual, and physical development. It is rather obvious that the educational and socio-economic background of the teacher enters here. She needs this understanding to be warm and accepting of all students and to establish rapport and a happy, productive environment. She needs to understand her own worth and the importance of her position, and to take pride in it. So many adults in our society are not aware of the vital need for, and importance of, early childhood education. So it must be part of the teacher's role to educate parents as well as students.

She needs a complete understanding of the necessity for socialization and enculturation because this is so much a part of the role we ascribe to her. She needs to promote a positive self-image in each individual child. She must appreciate and respect the pluralistic culture existing in American society.

Men In Early Childhood Classrooms

Throughout this book we have consistently referred to the teacher in the feminine gender. Are there any men at all in this field? Would it even be desirable to have men teaching and working with young children?

Indeed it is desirable. Part of socialization and enculturation involves the child's learning the appropriate sex role. For so many young children, a good male model is missing in their lives. Even in loving homes with two parents, fathers are often gone so much that a small boy has difficulty identifying with the father. Can you see what a man could do for children in the classroom?

The overwhelming number of teachers in this area are women, but a few men are entering the classrooms. Often this has been on an experimental basis to see how it would work. Much satisfaction has been expressed by men involved in such experimental situations. Men have been tried primarily in kindergartens, but, in several instances, young men are actively involved in teaching, or at least directing, nursery school or day care programs with very happy results. This, too, is one of those changing situations. We shall probably see more men participating in early childhood education in the future. One serious problem with attracting men into the field has been the low salaries traditionally paid to individuals employed in nursery schools, day care centers, and even public schools. Since these positions have been regarded as women's jobs, and the community has not viewed it as rewarding, important work, salaries have been very low. In order to attract high quality teachers of both sexes there must be greater financial rewards.

Children respond well to male teachers in early childhood.

Early Childhood Education For All

Much of the material presented in this chapter has emphasized the social and intellectual needs of the disadvantaged. You may wonder whether preschool education is necessary for all children. Can all children profit from early education, or is it only helpful to those disadvantaged children with marked language, and other, deficiencies?

This is a logical question to follow our discussion. Early childhood education should be a helpful and pleasurable experience for all children. The needs differ somewhat, but well-prepared teachers will understand this. All programs should be similar in that they help the child grow physically, mentally, socially, and emotionally. Early childhood education should never harm families and family life, rather it should support and strengthen the family in all instances.

National priorities with respect to achieving early childhood education for all are underscored in the following quotation from an article by former Senator John Tunney of California:

> We have cheerfully spent $23 billion on the space program. . . . The major tangible gains from men on the moon may not be apparent for a long time—maybe not until several more generations have been born, lived, argued, and died. But think of the possible gains from early schooling. A new generation of bright, bright kids. A steady withering away of the drop-out problem. A generation of intelligent, well-educated adults, equipped with the knowledge and skills necessary for survival and success in an ever more complicated world (9).

Senator Tunney evidently sees early childhood education as something of a panacea. It probably will not solve all our social and educational problems, but it might help a great deal to solve some of them.

Walter Mondale, while serving as Senator from Minnesota, along with Congressman Brandemas of Indiana, was very active in developing legislation for child care programs and in soliciting national support for such programs. Although the comprehensive Child Development Act of 1971 was vetoed by President Nixon on grounds that it would undermine the family and the family's authority in child rearing, Mondale and Brandemas continued to submit legislation and by 1975 the time was apparently right. The Child and Family Services Act was passed and signed into law by President Ford. The law provides for an Office of Children, Youth, and Family Services within HEW. Under this office fall a variety of responsibilities in overseeing day care and other family services. Head Start is also under this office at present.

In summarizing the key points of this chapter we can say that we are living in an era of dramatic change. One of the biggest factors affecting young children is the changing role of women in our society, particularly the entry of millions of mothers into the labor force. Many women need day care or nursery programs for their young children. The great number of women presently heading families also affects young children profoundly. Because of inadequate socialization, particularly in the area of language development, many compensatory programs that have been developed have placed heavy stress on language. Meeting the needs of young disadvantaged children must become the responsibility of the whole society. The national government as well as the local community must provide more and better care and education for all young children. Teacher education must be strengthened and more capable professionals, both men and women, must be recruited and adequately compensated.

Finally, we need to consider providing early childhood programs and parental help for all who wish it.

Our next chapter will deal with a few of the specifics of a good learning environment for young children.

References

1. *Statistical Abstract of the United States.* U.S. Dept. of Commerce, Bureau of Census, 1975.

2. Carro, Geraldine. "Who Says Our Children Never Had It So Good?" *Ladies' Home Journal*, July 1976, p. 38.

3. Carter, Hugh, and Glick, Paul. *Marriage and Divorce.* Cambridge, Mass.: Harvard University Press, 1976.

4. Howe, Louise K. *The Future of the Family.* New York: Simon and Schuster, 1972.

5. Webster, Loraine. "A Danish Experience." *The Elementary School Journal*, April 1975, pp. 419-21.

6. Deutsch, Martin et al., *The Disadvantaged Child.* New York: Basic Books, Inc., 1967.

7. Heimstra, Roger. *The Educative Community.* Lincoln, Nebraska: Professional Educators Publications, Inc., 1972.

8. King, Edith W., and Kerber, August. *The Sociology of Early Childhood Education.* New York: American Book Co., 1968.

9. Tunney, John Varick. "How Smart Do You Want Your Child To Be?" *McCall's*, October 1970, pp. 62ff.

SUPPLEMENTAL REFERENCES

1. Cave, William M., and Chesler, Mark A. *Sociology of Education.* New York: Macmillan Publishing Co., Inc., 1974.

2. Margolin, Edythe. *Sociocultural Elements of Early Childhood Education.* New York: Macmillan Publishing Co., Inc., 1974.

3. Rich, John M. *Challenge and Response: Education in American Culture.* New York: John Wiley and Sons, Inc., 1974.

Chapter 6

THE LEARNING ENVIRONMENT

The environment of early childhood education is determined, at least in part, by the purpose of the school. If it is a day care center the purpose may be primarily custodial care. In many of the programs for disadvantaged children the purpose is compensatory or remedial education. In traditional nursery schools the purpose has been developmental education. Most, however, are a combination of these purposes.

In all schools for young children the school must meet minimal standards set by state and local authorities. If the program is receiving federal funding it must also adhere to guidelines established by the sponsoring federal agency. Most of these standards or guidelines have to do with safety, adequate space, fire regulations, bathroom facilities, and the number of adults required to work with a given number of children.

The purpose and philosophy of the program have much to do with the actual school setting but, as in all schools, teachers are necessarily limited by fixed physical arrangements such as size, placement of doors, windows, storage space, and the like. There certainly must be areas for active indoor and outdoor play as well as areas for less strenuous activities. We will deal with these areas more specifically in the discussion of learning centers within the classroom. The school setting should be an environment for happy living and learning, with the school working as closely as possible with the home.

There is still quite a bit of public unease about the home and school relationship. The socialization of the child must take place, but ideally shouldn't much of this still occur in the home? How much do we want to turn over to the school? Our society (and our lawmakers) has shown great reluctance to turn over responsibilities traditionally considered as the prerogatives of parents. In fact, the total socialization of the child is the responsibility of varied social institutions. The family is most important, but the neighborhood, the church, the child's peer group, and the entire community play a part in the way each child is inducted into society.

Parental Involvement

The parent must hold primary responsibility for the teaching of the very young child. Nearly all the experimental intervention programs we outlined earlier make an intensive effort to involve parents. Some focus entirely on parents; they bring parents into the classroom as paraprofessionals or aides, or teachers make home visits to provide continuity of program from home to school. In various ways the parents are encouraged to participate, and an effort is made to create a mutual undertaking. Remember that these were primarily programs for disadvantaged children whose parents have often never taken an active role in their children's schooling, whereas middle-class parents have traditionally been very interested in their young children's education, and a close relationship has often existed between home and school. No educator would dispute the prior responsibility of the parent. Parents are certainly the best teachers of the very young child. When children do broaden their horizons and move into a school environment, it is vital that a good home/school relationship be maintained. Parents and teachers simply must work together for the welfare of the child. Ideally, the school should reinforce parental teaching and vice versa. Dr. Lillian Katz, an outstanding figure in the area of early childhood education, has enumerated eight needs of young children that must be met by both parents and teachers. Examining these will be helpful in determining the responsibilities of both teachers and parents toward young children.

First, children need optimum amounts of what is necessary for their well-being and wholesome development. Examples of this are attention and affection. Children must receive enough, yet too much of either can actually be harmful. Children need freedom to make decisions and become independent, but again too much freedom given to a very young child can be disastrous. Stimulation is another need which must be provided in just the right amount.

The second need is security. Children need to feel safe and protected. They need to feel that they belong. Home and school must work closely together to meet this need. The child must feel happy and comfortable in school and not have the fear of being abandoned by parents.

A third need is self-esteem. This is a tricky area because families and cultural groups vary tremendously in their criteria for measuring individual worth. Some families expect high academic achievements, others value athletic ability, while still others might stress musical or artistic abilities or even physical attractiveness. This is an area where the school must be particularly sensitive and aware of the family's expectations of the child.

Fourth on the list offered by Dr. Katz is the need to feel that life is purposeful, that it is meaningful and real. Many adults assume artificial, affected ways of speaking and working with children. Children have the right to be taken seriously and to feel their work is as real and important as is adults'. Their work should be given sincere, honest attention by parents and teachers.

The fifth need cited is adult help in making sense of the child's experiences. Again, both parents and teachers can help a child sort out the real from the unreal, the true from the untrue, aspects of living. Perhaps this is more urgent today when so many false claims are made constantly in advertising.

A sixth need is for adults who can accept and use the authority they have by virtue of being older, wiser, and more experienced. Teachers and parents must exercise power and authority with young children—but the power must be tempered with love and concern.

A seventh need is for good adult models. We have known for a long time that young children learn a great deal through imitation of those around them. We all need many models in our lives, but young children particularly need teachers who exemplify qualities children should learn. Along with this need is the eighth, which states that young children need relationships with adults who hold values that children will want to emulate. Too frequently today teachers are ambivalent about their own values. Children need both parents and teachers who value their own values (1).

The importance of home and school relationships can not be emphasized too strongly. If parents hold such an important teaching role in the lives of young children, how can teachers in a school situation provide a continuation of home teaching and help provide the "optimum" described above?

No school can take the place of a secure, loving home with parents who talk to their children, read to them, and provide many and varied cultural experiences. Yet we know from our earlier discussions that schools can offer much to a child to facilitate learning. How can a school create a bridge for the child to go back and forth from home learnings to school learnings which will be mutually reinforced? If a preschool or nursery school is comfortable, and a warm and a homelike atmosphere prevails, the child can easily make the transition from home to school and back again. A good early childhood classroom will accept children as they are, and children will have the necessary feelings of belonging. Although they will feel comfortable and "at home," the situation will be different enough to be stimulating. It will provide new, challenging experiences, but not frightening ones. It will provide the security of an easy, well-understood routine, but also scope for exploration and discovery by the child. This may sound too good to be true, but this kind of planned education is really possible. A good preschool program does provide all this, and more, for many children.

The Teacher

The child's first school experience should be very positive. Whether it is nursery school, day care, Head Start, kindergarten, or first grade, the teacher should be an exceptional one. In past years, these teaching positions were often regarded as of less importance than those for teaching older children. Now we know it takes talent, intelligence, and education of a very special kind to produce a fine teacher in early childhood education. The days are gone when it was thought that anyone who got on well with children could satisfactorily staff a classroom.

We need to stress that the teacher is the most important component of any educational program. The most beautiful, lavishly equipped physical plant is worthless if there is not a dynamic, exciting, interesting teacher in it. Some characteristics that the ideal teacher should embody can be cited. Naturalness and spontaneity are important. Creativity ranks high, as does resourcefulness, maturity, stability, and a professional attitude. Enthusiasm, flexibility, and a sense of humor are essential. This area of teaching is so vital that we can settle for nothing less than top people and top performance.

The Physical Plant

What of the physical environment? What is desirable? The physical environment is important, of course, but it is much less important than the teacher. A spacious room, or rooms, may be needed. Little children need plenty of room for active play. A pleasant outdoor play area should be an extension of the indoor school when weather permits. There should be lots of large muscle equipment both indoors and out. There should be a variety of toys, games, and manipulative materials. The overall appearance should be bright, colorful, and cheerful. We certainly want our children's earliest contacts with school to be made in an attractive surrounding. We want to see pictures and books that will appeal to the young and plenty of room to display children's work. We would expect to see a variety of audio-visual aids such as tape recorders, record players, film projectors, overhead projectors, filmstrip projectors, and a television set. Many other aids can be found in some modern classrooms.

We might add just a few more things about the physical equipment. Light-weight, sturdy, and comfortable furniture is a must. A rocking chair or two is a pleasant touch. Accessible bathroom facilities and sinks will provide a place for cleaning operations. Everything is, of course, geared to the size of the very young student. Some facilities for rest are usually needed, but this can be handled easily enough with folding cots or even a small rug on the floor. The rest period is more important in all-day programs. Traditionally, many early childhood programs for children under six have been only half-day classes.

Learning Centers

Another indication of a good learning environment is many learning centers. Learning centers of all types are assuming more importance in both preschool and elementary classrooms today. The list of centers which can be utilized is almost endless, but in a general way we can discuss some of those found quite frequently in schools for young children.

There will certainly be a housekeeping center. Here will be found toys to be used in "playing house", such as stoves, sinks, tables and chairs, cupboards, dishes, dolls, and anything else useful for this kind of role playing activity. There is often a "dress-up" box with many grown up clothes and accessories so children can assume different roles more easily.

A block center is commonplace. All sizes and shapes of blocks are useful and excellent for imaginary play. Much role playing goes on here too as houses, barns, garages, and even whole towns are constructed.

Wood working centers are seen frequently. Here potential carpenters and builders can use real hammers and saws to once again learn by imitating adult behavior.

Centers for water play are useful learning centers, as well as being fun. All young children like to splash and play in water. Very ingenious water tables are being constructed today just for classroom use. Water play offers

Role playing in "dress-up" clothes has always been part of childhood.

a great learning opportunity. Children learn about floating, sinking, measuring, density, volume, and more. Sand boxes or tables serve a similar function. The library center is also a must in the early childhood classroom. A table with lots of appealing picture story books on it may be all that is needed. Simply having a comfortable place to sit and enjoy books in a leisurely, quiet way is essential. This type of center is more elaborate in some schools today and includes such aids as tape recorders, film strip projectors, or even typewriters. Phonics and sound games or writing materials may be found in some centers too.

The Sand Table is a traditional learning center.

There is often an art center featuring easels, paints, clay, crayons, scissors, many kinds of paper and other art equipment. A music center will often focus on the piano in the classroom, but will also have the record player and rhythm instruments close at hand.

Science centers can be fascinating additions to the classroom. Here may be live animals such as rabbits, gerbils, or similar pets. Aquariums, terrariums, and displays that change frequently with seasons and interest can all be part of the science area.

Other centers may be cooking areas where real cooking and baking can occur. Listening centers are often incorporated into a program. Puzzle and game spots in the room may become still other learning centers. (2, pp. 219-230).

Learning centers for small children are limited only by space and the classroom inhabitants' imaginations.

The Schedule

How should a child spend his time in a preschool school or kindergarten classroom? We need to know a little about scheduling and the way time is allocated.

This varies a lot, and there may be almost as many different schedules as there are schools. We can give you only some very general ideas on scheduling practices. The first thing you must realize is the need for flexibility in scheduling. No timetable can be, or should be, adhered to too rigidly in an early childhood classroom. This holds true through the primary grades, but you do need a schedule because young children need the security and predictability of a routine. Your individual situation, your unique group of children and their needs, your particular problems, all these will combine to dictate the sort of schedule you will have. To give a better conception of the major time blocks to be set up, we can look at a daily schedule for a three- and four-year-old group.

9:00 - 9:15	Opening greetings, conversation time
9:15 - 10:00	Activity Period possible activities include wheeled toys, art activities, water or sand play, blocks, individual reading or math materials.
10:00 - 10:30	Outdoor Play
10:30 - 11:00	Snack Time

| 11:00 - 11:30 | Teacher guided activities: songs, rhymes, rhythms, fingerplays, and stories |
| 11:30 - 11:40 | Dismissal |

Cooking Centers are rewarding and interesting spots.

Listening Centers are frequently found in early childhood programs today.

Puzzle and Game Centers are often popular areas in the classroom.

This is really just suggestive of a daily routine. You could do any of these things or some things not even mentioned. Daily events have a way of modifying the schedule. A balance between active play, rest, and group and individual activities must be maintained, however.

The following are several suggested kindergarten schedules:

8:45 - 9:15	Arrival, outdoor play or free play indoors
9:15 - 9:30	Greetings, conversation, listening and planning
9:30 - 10:15	Work time
10:15 - 10:30	Clean up, evaluation
10:30 - 11:00	Outdoor play and rest
11:00 - 11:30	Music, listening, rhythms, games, story-time, and goodbyes
11:30 -	Dismissal

or:

9:00 - 9:15	Greetings, conversation, listening and planning
9:15 - 9:55	Group work, free play
9:55 - 10:10	Clean up, evaluation
10:10 - 10:35	Outdoor play, rest
10:35 - 11:30	Music, rhythms, games, library time, and goodbye

or:

12:45 - 1:30	Arrival, listening to conversation, and story telling
1:30 - 1:45	Rhythms and games
1:45 - 2:15	Outdoor play, rest
2:15 - 2:45	Music, listening, and dramatics

2:45 - 3:30	Planning and work time, clean up, and evaluation
3:30 -	Goodbye

or:

12:45 - 1:30	Arrival, free play, roll call, sharing and planning
1:30 - 2:00	Work period
2:00 - 2:15	Meeting, evaluation of work, listening and speaking
2:15 - 2:45	Outdoor play, rest
2:45 - 3:30	Library time, games, dramatization, music, telling stories, time for dictating stories
3:30 -	Goodbye (3)

The environment and the schedule must be flexible and provide for movement, some choice in activities, and comfortable routine. Planning an all-day program requires even more attention to scheduling to ensure adequate rest, nutrition, and appropriate activities.

We shall turn our attention to curriculum development next.

References

1. Katz, Lillian. "The Young Child in Focus," opening address presented to the National Conference of the Australian Preschool Association, Melbourne, Australia. May 1976.

2. Frost, Joe L. and Kissinger, Joan B. *The Young Child and the Educative Process.* New York: Holt, Rinehart and Winston, 1976.

3. *A Guide for Kindergarten Teachers.* Sioux Falls Public Schools, S.D.

SUPPLEMENTAL REFERENCES

1. Brophy, Jere E.; Good, Thomas L.; and Nedler, Shari E. *Teaching in the Preschool.* New York: Harper and Row, Publishers, 1975.

2. Hildebrand, Verna. *Introduction to Early Childhood Education.* New York: Macmillan Publishing Co., 1976.

3. Widmer, Emmy L. *The Critical Years: Early Childhood Education at the Crossroads.* Scranton, Pa.: International Textbook Co., 1970.

Chapter 7

CURRICULUM
DEVELOPMENT

T he curriculum is the total coursework offered by an educational institution. With kindergarten and primary grade children, whom we include in the definition of early childhood, the curriculum has been rather well established. Quite a lot of controversy continues over methods and materials, but no one would dispute the need for children to learn to read and write. Probably the question *when* is the most debatable. How much reading and writing should be taught in kindergarten?

What of the curriculum for children prior to kindergarten? Here, rather than limiting ourselves to thinking about courses and subject areas, most teachers in early childhood education prefer to consider curriculum as everything that happens to children at school. This includes organized (and often disorganized) play, informal talk, or eating lunch, as well as the learning experiences specifically planned by the teacher. All experience is learning for the young child. Part of the child's small, but expanding, world is the teacher and the school. How do teachers build on this to create an appropriate curriculum for young children?

One of the first things to consider in curriculum planning is the initial purpose of the school. Why are parents enrolling their children in this particular school? For example, Head Start programs have been deliberately designed to promote cognitive abilities in disadvantaged children in order to help these children catch up with their more advantaged peers before entering kindergarten or first grade. Most private nursery schools are created to provide enrichment experiences. Generally, such nursery schools are half-day situations intended to broaden the already rich learning environment of the middle-class child. The prime purpose of day care centers is usually to provide quality care to children whose parents are working or otherwise unable to care for them during the day. It has only been relatively recently that day care has included planned educational experiences as part of the program.

So, in planning curriculum, one should first consider the focus of the particular early childhood program. What do parents want and expect from the program?

Organized play is part of the early childhood curriculum.

Social learnings are acquired through play.

Eating lunch can be considered part of the curriculum and should be a planned learning experience.

Learning Theory

Another important consideration in planning the curriculum is the question of how young children learn best and what is the most effective teaching approach.

Those who subscribe to the teaching of B.F. Skinner and other behaviorists would adhere closely to the stimulus-response style of teaching by strongly reinforcing desired behavior. One writer who advocates this style of education for young children has set down seven steps for modifying behavior as follows:

1. Human behavior can be changed at any age.

2. Environment can change behavior.

3. An individual can develop the ability to change not only his own behavior but that of others.

4. The environment has its greatest effect when a behavior is in its most rapid stage of development.

5. Most human behavior is sequential in development. That is, a new behavior is based on similar behavior that preceded it in development.

6. Often it is easier to learn a new behavior than to erase old behavior and replace it with new.

7. Instruction in the prekindergarten is most effective and economical (in terms of time and effort) when learning activities are planned and implemented to bring about desired behavior change in the child (1, p. 4).

Planning the curriculum from this point of view would involve using behavioral objectives or stating the specific behavioral changes expected from a certain lesson. In other words, the teacher plans to provide an experience (teaching) that will make a specific change in the child. A particular, measurable learning will be the result of the planned experience or lesson.

Tightly structured programs such as E-B (DISTAR) follow behavioral learning theory. A curriculum of this sort might be one in which physical activities are not included in the overall curriculum plan. Although the need for physical education is recognized, educators adhering to this theory might concern themselves more with cognitive learning and expect other aspects of the child's development to take care of themselves. The E-B program, for example, is heavily oriented toward reading, language, and math, and such curricular areas as physical education, the arts, and social development are not emphasized. Block building and easel painting might not be incorporated into the curriculum for three- and four-year-olds in this type of program. Creative activities would not be strongly stressed.

At the opposite end of the continuum are traditional or developmental curricular programs for young children. Perhaps it should be clarified here that the term "traditional" in the area of early childhood education does not have the same connotation that it has in elementary and secondary education. The very words "traditional education" evoke a picture of an authoritarian teacher in a formal classroom with the desks in orderly rows. In the context of early childhood education traditional means the developmental point of view in which the total development of the child is of concern in planning the curriculum. Social and emotional development, as well as cognitive growth, is emphasized. In this kind of curriculum Piaget's ideas may be stressed in which it is believed that children learn through total experience as they progress through natural, developmental stages of learning. Play is viewed as an integral part of the curriculum. Social learnings are important, as is creative activity. Much more time will be spent in unstructured, spontaneous activity.

As has already been indicated, the dozens of different model programs range from the first example used to the second. Obviously, in addition to understanding the purpose or focus of the school one must understand the philosophy of learning in order to achieve a degree of consistency in curriculum planning. The behaviorist approach to curriculum for the young child has been referred to as adult-centered while the developmentalists have often been called child-centered, but in actuality most programs combine elements of both points of view. Most educators are middle-of-the-roaders and see advantages to children working, learning, and growing in varied situations. Some activities will be more teacher-directed and some will be free choices for the child. Providing for individual needs, letting children have concrete learning experiences where they can learn inductively through problem solving situations, and fostering positive self-images are all quite important in curriculum planning.

A balance is needed between active and quiet times and among the various subject areas. This balance should permit emphasis on social, physical, and intellectual development. A writer in the area of curriculum has offered the following list of guidelines to aid in arriving at a balanced curriculum. Children need:

1. To succeed and to feel worthy,

2. To share in making decisions and in accepting responsibilities,

3. To develop values and behaviors consistent with democratic living,

4. To develop problem solving skills,

5. To explore the natural environment,

6. To develop routines and habits that facilitate positive social living and enhance personal well being (for example, sharing materials, cleaning up materials after their use, and washing hands before eating),

7. To be active and to rest, to interact with others and to be alone,

8. To improve communications skills,

9. To expand expressive skills in art, music, movement, and dramatic play,

10. To develop comprehensive sensorimotor skills (for example, acquiring large and small motor skills),

11. To establish conceptual foundations in mathematics, science, and the social sciences (2, p. 83).

The age and maturity of young children are also very important in planning. A common error made by inexperienced staff members is expecting four-year olds in a school situation to act like six- or even eight-year olds. As Hymes has repeatedly informed us in his writings, young children are not good sitters, rather they are active learners (3, pp. 36-38). It is quite unrealistic to expect young children to sit quietly for any long period of time. The same teaching materials are not appropriate for three-year olds and seven-year olds, and obviously, very young children don't cope well with formal academic lessons. Teachers accustomed to working with older elementary children may make the mistake of trying to teach young children in the way they taught fourth grade. It doesn't work.

There should also be an awareness that the curriculum for the young child is not confined to the classroom and playground. Learning about his world means seeing and doing many things outside the school. Visiting a farm or a fire station, a bakery, the public library, the zoo, an airport, or simply taking a walk to the park will broaden understandings about the community and the world. Learning about the work, the interdependence of people, and just how things happen or function is part of the early childhood curriculum.

There must also be built-in planning for special occasions. Holidays such as Halloween, Christmas, Valentine's Day, and even each child's birthday must be duly noted and celebrated. The first day of school is very important as is the last day. All these special days and occasions must be systematically incorporated into the curriculum.

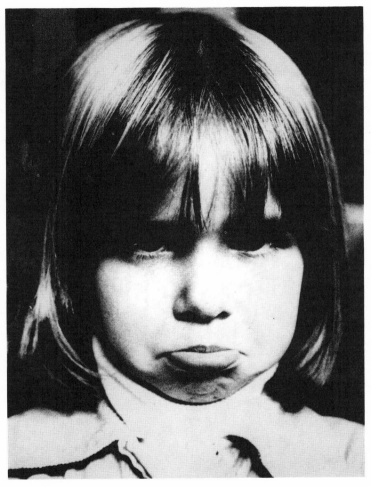

Humanistic, child-centered curricula help children accept their feelings and learn to deal with them.

Evaluation

Continuous evaluation both of the larger goals of the schools and of daily lessons or activities is essential. The teacher will better understand her responsibilities and the accomplishments of the total program if ongoing evaluation takes place. It is also an aid in daily planning and modification of teaching—and teachers do need to continually modify their teaching. If a lesson or activity does not succeed in producing the desired results, perhaps a different approach will succeed the next time. Staff discussions of what worked well and what did not, evaluations by superiors, or simply individual self-assessment can all be helpful. All teachers need to question themselves as to why a certain lesson is successful while another is a total fiasco. The overall goals need to be kept in mind. Are the children achieving the desired results? Are parents pleased? Is the program effective?

The teacher's evaluation of her own work is important, but individual and group evaluation of children is also essential. Both formal and informal evaluations take place. Formal evaluation can be done by check lists, reports to parents, anecdotal and other records, and conferences. All of this evaluation will eventually be used in curriculum planning.

Major and minor revisions in curriculum need to take place frequently. We should think of curriculum as a continuous process rather than as something set and established in a final form.

In summarizing this discussion of curriculum planning, a listing of the major concerns presented should be helpful:

1. The major purpose or function of the school must be given attention.

2. The learning theory to which you adhere decidedly influences curriculum planning.

3. A balance in curriculum areas and variety of activities is needed.

4. The ages and developmental stages of children are important elements in curriculum planning.

5. Children's special needs and interests must be given attention in planning.

6. Continuous evaluation of children's progress and of the total educational effort, including teaching, is also a part of curriculum planning.

7. There should be flexibility and scope for creativity.

8. Curriculum is a dynamic process which is constantly changing.

Careful curriculum planning is essential. In the following chapters more discussion of specific curriculum areas will be presented. It should be noted that the curriculum material presented is quite traditional; that is, it is the conventional type of program that has been most accepted in early childhood education.

References

1. Vance, Barbara. *Teaching the Prekindergarten Child: Instructional Design and Curriculum.* Monterey, California: Brooks/Cole Publishing Company, 1973.

2. Hipple, Marjorie L. *Early Childhood Education Problems and Methods.* Pacific Palisades, California: Goodyear Publishing Company, Inc., 1975.

3. Hymes, James L. *Teaching the Child Under Six.* Columbus, Ohio: Charles E. Merrill Publishing Company, 1974.

SUPPLEMENTAL REFERENCES

1. Eliason, Carol F., and Jenkins, Loa T. *A Practical Guide to Early Childhood Curriculum.* St. Louis, Missouri: The C. V. Mosby Co., 1977.

2. Margolin, Edythe. *Young Children, Their Curriculum and Learning Processes.* New York: Macmillan Publishing Co., Inc., 1976.

3. Robison, Helen F. *Exploring Teaching in Early Childhood Education.* Boston: Allyn and Bacon, Inc., 1977.

Chapter 8

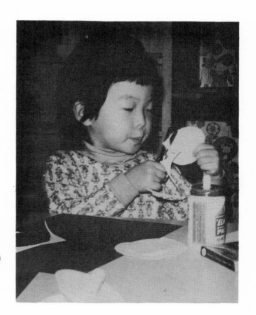

THE CURRICULUM

W e have mentioned the language arts frequently because the importance of language development in these early years cannot be overstressed. Although we have emphasized the necessity of language enrichment for disadvantaged preschoolers, a great deal of high quality language arts instruction is necessary in all early childhood programs. The language arts are the cement that holds programs together. They are the first and foremost aspect of any early childhood curriculum.

Just what is included under the term "language arts"? Ordinarily we would list listening, speaking, reading, and writing. These would be broken down into such areas as oral expression, practical and creative writing, spelling, handwriting, literature, grammar, and usage. When you include all these elements the total amount of time that is involved with language arts activities during a school day is a very high percentage. Since most preschool children don't read, there must be a great deal of oral communication between teacher and child. An estimated 80 or 90 percent of the very young child's time is taken up with listening, speaking, conversational give-and-take, individual and group oral expression, prereading or writing activities, or, in some cases, actually working on beginning reading and writing. Any area of the curriculum which involves language in any way, from math to music, is also part of the language arts program.

The teacher obviously needs to provide an excellent model in the use of language. Speaking with clear and accurate articulation is a part of this model. Usage should conform to generally accepted standards, and even the quality of the teacher's voice is important. A pleasant, well-modulated speaking voice is essential.

Literature

Under the general heading of literature are poetry, verse, and rhymes. Sometimes children will say them chorally; sometimes they will just listen. The Mother Goose rhymes so dear to all children are a part of literature. Another kind of rhyme children enjoy tremendously is the finger play. There are literally hundreds of these, and children can become totally engrossed in acting out these little plays. Many other incidental learnings take place, too, such as numerical concepts. Nonsense verse, chants, even singing games are also a part of literature. Stories, read or told, are an important part, of course, and often they are dramatized with pictures or flannel board representations. Stories may be taped, and the child can listen as often as he likes to a favorite story and follow along in the book at the same time. You can see how this would facilitate reading readiness. Puppetry can make stories come alive in a vivid manner, too. Dramatics often happen as the result of favorite stories. Nearly all children love acting out "The Three Bears" or "Little Red Riding Hood." Sometimes dramatic play takes another form, too—creative role playing. If a child fears a new experience such as going to a dentist, we can frequently alleviate his worry by demonstrating through creative role playing just what is going to happen. You can see that literature provides limitless opportunities for language development. Many positive experiences with literature at this time cannot help but encourage very young children to love and enjoy books and stories. Perhaps there is no single more important activity that a parent or teacher can do than read stories to a child as often as possible. A shared enjoyment of books goes a long way toward encouraging a later love of reading. Besides instilling a love of books and stories, reading also helps increase the speaking vocabulary.

Listening And Speaking

Probably the language activities we all engage in most frequently are listening and speaking, and children are no exception. The listening that very young children do determines their language patterns in large measure. They absorb words like a sponge, easily acquiring verbal skill and proficiency. As noted earlier, the Montessori schools and others, too, often capitalize on this prime time for language development to teach a second language.

A tape recorder is a useful tool here. Children can learn much by hearing how they sound on tape because listening and oral expression go hand in hand, all conversational give-and-take involves both. This kind of informal interaction is going on constantly between teacher and child, or among children themselves throughout the school day. In a little more formal way some oral expression takes place in class or small group discussions, in "Show and Tell" time, in choral speaking, and in sharing or reporting information one child has acquired. Finger plays and dramatics would, of course, employ oral speech frequently.

Children need many opportunities for oral expression. Finger plays develop listening and speaking skills.

THE CURRICULUM

Handwriting And Spelling

It can easily be seen how all these experiences take place as part of the daily routine in an early childhood program, but what about some of the other aspects of language arts? Do skills like handwriting and spelling have any place in a classroom for very young children?

Surprisingly enough, the answer to that would have to be yes. Handwriting, for example, may not be formally taught to very young children, but many prewriting activities can take place. Children at this age learn to hold pencils and crayons. They draw and trace. They outline and color. Their coordination becomes increasingly fine as they practice with these implements of writing. Many children actually seek instruction in handwriting as they become a little more mature. It is not at all unusual for a four-year old to exhibit great interest in writing his own name and perhaps other familiar words. Often by kindergarten the young child is ready for some formal instruction in handwriting. In many kindergarten classrooms the children write the entire alphabet in manuscript and some become quite proficient. This should not be forcefully imposed, and it usually is not. Quite often, young children, given a choice of activities, will select a writing activity. Obviously, if they are going to write they must learn the letters, and so this becomes a reading readiness experience as well. There is really no separation between reading and writing; they are as inextricably related as listening and speaking. Some even think that handwriting needs to precede reading because the encoding of language enables decoding to occur.

To further demonstrate how integrated instruction is in early childhood classes, consider the use of alphabet letters as part of art activities. There are many kinds of alphabet letters that children can manipulate. Sets of felt and sandpaper letters can help children add to their reading and writing skills while they trace these textured letters with their fingers. Montessori did a great deal of experimenting that indicates that tactile and kinesthetic experiences such as these are real aids to learning with some children.

Incidental learnings in spelling go along with writing. Spelling is never taught as a formal spelling lesson, but, because children begin to learn to recognize and write letters, they are often interested in how to put letters together to make words. Usually the child's name is the first thing he evinces an interest in spelling. (Remember Piaget's teaching concerning the egocentricism of the young child.) The wise teacher will capitalize on the knowledge that practical, concrete, egocentric learnings are most successful with very young children.

Fine motor coordination and prewriting skills are developed in early childhood.

Grammar And Usage

Formal grammar is not taught in early childhood education classrooms, but usage is taught. By providing the desirable teacher model we spoke of earlier, the child will absorb much about language usage. Teaching standard usage to disadvantaged children or children with strong dialects, is almost like teaching a new language. The child uses standard usage for school, and returns to his dialect at home. Some bilingual children have problems, but it is amazing how well many of them manage their double language life.

Creative And Practical Writing

We usually don't associate practical writing activities such as writing letters or reports with small children, but they actually do more in this area than one would suspect. Children do create composite letters of various types such as invitations and thank you notes. Most of their practical and creative writing is dictated to someone else who possesses the necessary writing skill. Nevertheless, it is writing. In addition, they make lists when engaging in planning sessions and they label things. Even the ability to write one's name is an example of practical writing, and a name put on papers and art work enhances that all important self-concept we have alluded to so many times. It is a part of each child's learning his own unique identity.

Practical writing is the kind we all do most frequently because it is necessary for getting along in our society. It is useful for the young child, too, and becomes more so as he discovers the uses of written language and its power to communicate his thought.

There is no clear-cut distinction between practical and creative writing. Rather, they overlap as do all language arts activities. For instance, although labeling is a practical writing activity, it can also be a creative one if the child comes up with a new idea. Composing captions for drawings may be highly creative, particularly as they increase in length, becoming a paragraph, then several paragraphs, developing into original stories in the process.

The experience story, one based on the child's own real or imagined experience, is the most meaningful kind of creative writing in which he engages. This has important implications for reading. It is actually a method of teaching beginning reading known as "the language experience approach." In this approach, after the child has dictated his own story, and the teacher or other adult helper has written it in manuscript form, often on large sheets of paper, the child can then begin to decode his own words. At the end of this chapter, you will find specific examples of language experience stories that can aid in fostering self-esteem.

Reading

Reading for the child under six was thought for a long period to be inadvisable, perhaps even physically damaging. "Reading Readiness" was what children were to have until the magic age of six. However, these ideas have been largely discredited, and many researchers have taken a serious look at when and how children can and do learn to read. For example, Delores Durkin, a noted student of the whole reading process, has found many children reading before school entry and, further, many of these children are virtually self-taught. She has called them "pencil and paper kids." They are children intrigued with words who often want to master letters and words by being able to write them. In the process they learn to decode written language by first learning how to encode it (1).

With this new awareness of the ability of some young children to master reading and prereading skills, many schools have begun teaching reading in kindergarten or even earlier. Because of this it is important that students concerned with early childhood education know some of the reading approaches most frequently used with young children. The proliferation of materials, programs, and gadgetry in the field of reading in recent years makes it virtually impossible to keep informed about all new developments. We will, however, look briefly at some of the better known approaches.

Basal Reader Approach

The traditional basal reader is still probably the most common way of teaching children to read. Its use involves learning a sight vocabulary of whole words, and, after mastery of sufficient sight words, beginning to read simple material. The basal series do get into phonics, but not until the child has the satisfaction of being able to identify a sizable number of words by sight. This method has received a great deal of criticism in recent years. Nonetheless, a remarkable number of children have learned to read in this way. "Dick and Jane" are now gone from the educational scene, but many reading series today still employ the technique made familiar by those famous basal readers.

Language-Experience Approach

Another approach frequently used with very young readers is the language-experience method previously mentioned in our discussion of writing. The idea here is to let children use their own experience, and consequently their own vocabulary, to learn to read. They write (or dictate) their own stories following Durkin's finding that encoding prior to decoding is an

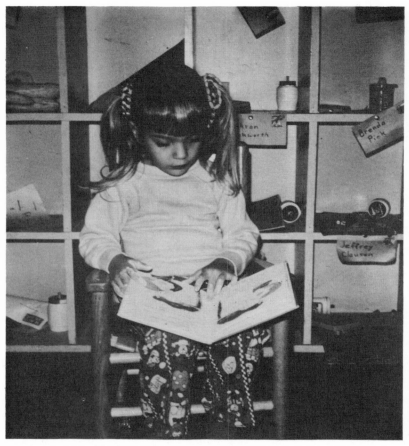

Extensive experience with books and stories is essential to successful later reading.

effective means of learning to read. This, too, involves whole word recognition, but since it is so closely related to the individual child's experience it is thought to be more meaningful to the child. The "key-word" approach espoused by Jeanette Veatch ties in with language experience. Words meaningful to the child are written down and, after they can consistently recognize them, the words become their own. They must keep building and acquiring these personal words until they actually have a considerable reading vocabulary (2).

Phonetic And Linguistic Approaches

There are a few completely phonetic approaches to beginning reading. In these the child learns phonetic sounds of letters separately and in combinations. He must then learn to associate the sounds with printed graphemes and sound out the printed word.

Another even newer approach is the linguistic reader in which emphasis is put on word families, with some rather unlikely stories resulting in order to incorporate large numbers of rhyming or related words.

Programmed Reading

Programmed reading for very young children also has its adherents. Here, in small sequential steps, children meet letters, sounds, and words. As they proceed through the programmed "frames" they are required constantly to make responses indicating their mastery of the reading material. These materials are self-correcting so the young reader can do much work independently. He is constantly tested and recycled through material he has not mastered adequately.

Initial Teaching Alphabet

Another interesting idea in teaching reading is the British import I.T.A. in which new symbols have been created to match all the sounds, resulting in an alphabet of forty-four letters. This augmented alphabet does seem to provide a true sounds-symbol approach, eliminating many inconsistencies in learning to read the English language. Children are taught only sounds, not letter names. It has been used with a high degree of success in some schools, both in England and the United States. There are some questions about the ultimate value of I.T.A., since the child does have to make the transition to traditional orthography in rather short time.

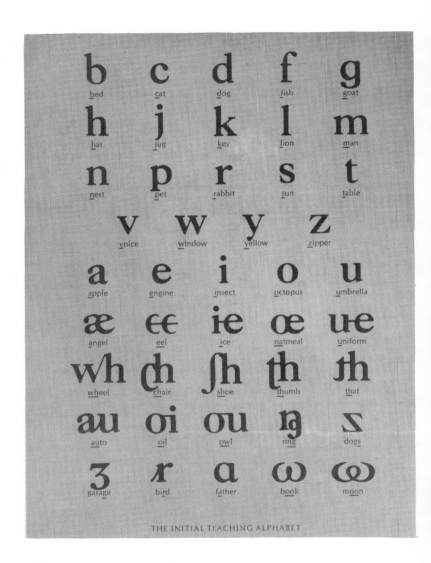

THE INITIAL TEACHING ALPHABET

Distar

DISTAR is both a program and a method which grew out of the work of Engleman and others (see pp. 19 and 23). They have attempted to develop reading (and math and language) materials particularly appropriate for disadvantaged preschool and primary grade children. This has been a highly controversial approach which employs some practices many educators deem questionable since it is totally teacher-dominated, highly structured, and features intensive drill with small groups. The lack of creative activities and teacher freedom is deemed unfortunate by some.

The actual method of teaching reading involves letter sounds being taught and then put together as, for example, in the word "cat." The children learn to say the separate sounds as k-k-k, aah, t-t-t. They will then be told to "say it fast." In order to do this they must recognize the letters and understand the corresponding sound. They then must understand that these sounds can be sequenced into a word by saying them fast.

Confusing aspects such as capitals and silent letters are not learned at first. In words with a silent e on the end, the e appears in a very small, almost unnoticeable form and gradually, as children progress through the materials, the e becomes larger and larger until it is the same size as the other letters.

In the early stages children learn a number of words through rhyming. Using the example "cat" again, the teacher will ask what word rhymes if you begin with b-b-b. Capitals and irregular words are introduced only after they have a sizable reading vocabulary.

Curriculum Integration

Language skills cannot be fragmented and taught in isolation. The following is a list of language activities that you might observe in any classroom filled with children from ages two to eight. Do you see how a variety of interrelated language skills could emanate from these activities? Do you see how they can relate to other areas of the curriculum?

Talking

Discussing

Story telling

Listening to literary selections, prose, and poetry

Playing games

Making lists of words—such as weather words, color words, holiday words, etc.

Dramatizations

Role playing

Pantomime

Naming and labeling things

Critical listening experiences

Films, film strips, slides

Authoring stories and poems

Classification activities

Using geometric shapes

Sensory experiences: smell, touch, taste

Prewriting and writing activities: circles and lines which make up all manuscript letters

Alphabet recognition activities: songs, games, kinesthetic play

Prereading and reading activities

James Hymes, who has long been recognized as an outstanding figure in early childhood education, puts forth his philosophy very convincingly in his book, *Teaching the Child Under Six*. He discusses his conception of what the curriculum should be for the young child by making an analogy with the liberal arts curriculum at the college level. According to him, we should strive for the same kind of balance in early childhood education in which the child has the opportunity to pursue the social sciences, the humanities, and the physical sciences (3). It is an interesting way to think about curriculum and may give some perspective on the whole area. Language arts are a vital part of any program, but we don't want to give the impression that other aspects of the curriculum are negligible.

Mathematics

We are aware that mathematics plays an important part in the young child's life, both in and out of school. Accurately, Piaget speculates:

> It is a great mistake to suppose that a child acquires the notion of numbers and other mathematical concepts just from teaching. On the contrary, to a remarkable degree he develops them himself, independently and spontaneously (4, p. 406).

Children hear and use measurement words in everyday language. Some examples are: little, big, taller, shorter, smaller, smallest, fatter, thinner, half, and whole. Measurement concept building begins in the home and should be capitalized on in the school. The parent who asks the child "do you want a half piece of bread or a whole piece?" not only begins the task of building whole number concepts, but fractional number concepts as well. The teacher should develop a list of measurement words and use them frequently in helping the child learn how language is used to compare objects.

The skill of estimating often parallels the activities a child experiences with measurement words. Adult-sized tables, for example, are all about the same height. In the later years of early childhood, when inches are understood, the generalizations on the sameness of table height can be expressed as thirty inches. Weight measures and estimates should receive similar attention—whether it be a pound of butter or a pound of hamburger that is used as the reference point. Balance scales should be in the classroom. Using the knowledge we have of the self-centered interest of young children in their own height and weight, we should make the necessary tools available to extend these measurement concepts.

A few comments about metric measurement should be included in this discussion. Spodek in his book, *Teaching in the Early Years* (5, pp. 166-167), suggests that both the English system of measurement and the metric system should be introduced to the child quite early. They should be presented as two different ways of measuring things. The rationale behind this is quite simple. We will probably be using both systems for many years to come. Children will need to learn we buy some liquids in liters and some in quarts, or that in some situations we measure length in meters but in others, yards. What should *not* be done is to emphasize conversion from one system to the other. That is awkward and unnecessary. It is simpler to familiarize children with both systems so they can use whichever one is appropriate.

In a university affiliated nursery school, children were observed recently measuring plant growth with a meter stick. The children had no problem with this and readily understood how many millimeters their plants had grown since they had last measured them.

Since preschool and primary grade children have not acquired knowledge of the old system to impede their acceptance of metric measurement, it appears that learning about both is a reasonable solution.

Properties of groups or sets have their beginnings in early childhood. One of the first familiar sets is the child's toys that may include subsets of blocks, model cars, dolls, etc. Set notions can be further extended when the child realizes that the blocks are made up of blocks of varying dimensions, colors, lengths, and shapes. Set notions can be reinforced through books—either read to the child or read by the child, depending upon language development. An example of such a book is *This Is My Family* (6). This book treats a circus family as a set and includes subsets of parents, children, maleness, femaleness, and dogs. Groups, subgroups, and intersection of sets are forcefully dealt with by the author.

There are many opportunities for children to have successful experiences in counting and developing the one-to-one correspondence of number to object. When a child responds to the frequently asked adult question "How old are you?" by hiding his thumb and holding up four fingers and saying "I am this many years old," the progress in conceptual thought is more advanced than if the parroted response of "I am four years old" were given. If the child can count serially the four fingers, advancement is even greater. Whether children have one-to-one correspondence experiences in the home or school is not important; it is important that they have them. The wise parent will provide the child with opportunities to place a carton of a dozen eggs in the storage tray of the refrigerator. The

Classification and mathematical set concepts have their beginnings in early childhood.

creative teacher will provide opportunities for children to distribute such common items as paper, pencils, scissors, and other materials to classmates. In either case should there be "one left over" we extend the child into why, and discovery, and decision making.

Placing the abstract symbols of mathematics in the child's memory bank is a difficult task. Calendars, clocks, numbered blocks, and other materials have value in the beginning. To omit the chalkboard and paper would be a mistake, since they are appropriate tools to assist children in communicating with numbers.

We should be familiar with the difficulties in learning to understand concepts of time. Christmas and birthdays never come, and a visit to the hospital for a needed operation may be too soon for some children. Time that is important to them is the key to conceptualization. School time, television time, and recess time, are examples of time significant to children. Telling time should be practiced.

We would be unwise to conclude that only the topics of geometric shapes, measurement, estimating, fractions, whole numbers, counting, properties of groups, one-to-one correspondence, and telling time are the mathematical curriculum for early childhood. This treatment is only the beginning. The fundamental operations of adding, subtracting, dividing, and multiplying, and the abstract symbolism involved with them, are a part

Counting pieces of candy has high appeal to young children.

of early education. A wide selection of textbooks and other print and manipulative materials is available to teachers in extending the mathematics curriculum. The teacher's knowledge of how children learn as well as possession of mathematical knowledge is of extreme importance. In summation, the mathematical curriculum in early childhood education should be characterized as self-discovery oriented, self-paced, and creative in nature, with many and diverse manipulative materials.

Science

The nature of the science curriculum is similar to that of mathematics because math and science are interrelated as the young child continually seeks answers posed by the environment.

Even though science does not appear in a completely organized way to the young child, several instrumental skills have their beginnings in early childhood education. To enumerate these skills we might include observation, experimentation, use of imagination, discussion, hypothesis making, and reading. Emphasis in developing these skills should be on interrelationships rather than separate entities. A prime goal of science is seeking truth.

At a very early age children observe that there are plants, animals, and inanimate objects in the environment. As they progress in their observation they begin to classify animals with fur, feathers, hard coverings, cool and warm to touch. Ultimately they will raise questions such as, where does the water go when it is observed leaving the sink, or, where do birds put their legs when they fly? It should be the parents' and teachers' function to maintain and encourage the imagination and curiosity that is innate to the child.

Simple experiments under the leadership of the teacher may include the chemical and texture changes involved in cooking, the physical changes involved in melting ice or snow, and growth changes of plants and animals. Discussion as to what happens in cooking, melting of ice, and growth of living things should be a part of science learning. Some hypothesis making may also be a part of experimentation. The often-used activity of plant growth in sunlight, less sunlight, and no sunlight can lead to science concept building.

The attitude of parent or teacher in building a love of science is directly related to developing the child's potential. When the small child brings the "sand toad" into the kindergarten classroom with the question "What is it" will he be received by the teacher with "Take it outside" or "Let's see if we can find out about it"?

Observation and experimentation lead to self-discovery.

Many children's books are available to strengthen the truths of the world of science. The teacher's vocabulary should be filled with "find," "describe," "make," "do," "measure," and similar words in order to extend the inquiring mind (7, p. 7). The attitude of building toward concepts, rather than facts, should be adopted by the teacher.

Art And Music

The aesthetic areas of art and music are also extremely important and can be related to all other aspects of curriculum. They are another avenue of communication that helps children become more creative and express themselves more completely. They are also areas of great enjoyment.

Early childhood teachers have often been supportive in these areas. Children have been encouraged to be creative, to use a wide variety of art media, and to acquire a keener awareness of the world and its wonders through art and music experiences. Most early childhood classrooms will have vivid and colorful displays of children's art work, and music and art centers are prominent parts of the room. It is difficult to imagine a classroom for young children without a piano, a record player, and an easel.

Art activities include such materials and activities as clay or similar manipulative materials, crayons, tempera paint, finger painting, and collages of paper, cloth, or other materials.

The sensitive teacher can discover much about children's development from their art work. Two experts, Victor Lowenfeld and W. Lambert Brittain, have systematized analysis of art work to determine stages of child development. Lowenfeld and Brittain indicated that the scribbling stage usually lasts from ages two to four. A preschemetic stage is generally found in the four to six period, and an early expressive stage starts about age six (8, pp. 89-144). The teacher or parent needs to delve into the writings of these two authorities to acquire an understanding of this type of developmental growth. Lowenfeld and Brittain have made a fascinating contribution to the fuller understanding of children.

Musical activities should include listening, creative movement to music, singing, and even acting out or dramatizing songs. Children can express creativity in rhythms and by using simple rhythm instruments. Singing games are also frequently played both in and out of school.

We need to remember that these experiences, besides enhancing the appreciation of both art and music, should be fun.

Health And Physical Education

Physical education and health cannot be overlooked in any overview of the curriculum for the young child. Physical education should aid in physical development and overall coordination. It should promote the general well-being of the child, and at times can even provide an emotional release. Children in the early childhood stages are rapidly mastering physical skills as well as learning the cooperative behavior necessary in many group games.

Children need a tremendous amount of vigorous activity of both the organized and informal types. They also need frequent changes in activity. Much of the physical activity should be outdoors, if at all possible.

Children need equipment on which to ride, climb, slide, and swing. They need balls of all sizes to develop ball handling skills. Balance beams are an increasingly common feature in early childhood classrooms. All the old, familiar, circle folk games are still useful. They need practice in hopping, skipping, jumping, and running (9).

There is truth in the saying, "Play is the child's work," because much learning ensues from these play activities.

Health teaching is often incidental, but nonetheless important. Teachers need to stress cleanliness, good nutrition, the necessity of sleep and exercise, appropriate clothing for the weather, and the role of doctors and dentists in preventative health care. Much of this can be done through stories,

Many types of
physical activity
are needed.

Gross motor
development is
essential.

99   THE CURRICULUM

pictures and posters, discussions, and actual classroom visitors. The school nurse and doctor can be invaluable allies, helping children to acquire positive attitudes toward healthful living. Dental exams can provide occasions for discussions of good care of the teeth. Safety rules are also important. They may be one of the earliest health matters and one of the most vital.

Here again, parental help and cooperation is essential. Much health teaching must be reinforced in the home if it is to have lasting effectiveness, a further reason for working closely with parents.

Social Studies

The teaching of social studies is receiving greater emphasis in today's world of cultural pluralism. The primary purpose in teaching social studies to young children is to bring about an understanding of self and others. All kinds of people must learn to live and work together and develop understanding and appreciation of one another.

The subject area accepted as social studies today includes all disciplines commonly known as the social sciences, including history, geography, anthropology, economics, sociology, government, and elements of psychology.

Social studies should help the child learn about social living and adjusting in groups of varied cultural backgrounds. Further, it should expand the child's curiosity about the world and people in it.

Social studies units for young children should be very brief, and several may be going on simultaneously. Often they will grow out of the child's interest. Work on self-esteem may come first, but following closely are topics such as the family, and neighborhood or community. These, of course, also help with development of a positive self-concept by enabling the child to understand how he fits in the society

Other commonly used topics in the area of social studies are the school, the zoo, the farm, community helpers, holidays, transportation, and the world of work. All of these can be seen as an extension of the egocentrism of the young child.

Career education is receiving new emphasis even with extremely young children. In looking at the work performed by fathers and mothers, children see an extension of themselves and their place in the community and society. So this, too, encourages the notion of positive self-concept. Techniques of teaching such social studies units include stories, poems, pictures, films and film strips, bulletin board displays, interest centers, and discussions.

Community resources should be widely used. Field trips to farms, police and fire stations, public libraries, retail and wholesale businesses, zoos, and many other similar visits can greatly augment the child's concrete knowledge of the immediate environment and the broader community.

The social studies curriculum must provide an integrated experience that is relevant to the life of the young child. It cannot be fragmented, nor rigid, nor too highly structured. The preceding are only suggestions as to what could be incorporated in a program. Some areas will need more or less emphasis depending on the needs of the children and community.

* * *

Suggested Language Experience Ideas To Enhance The Self-Concept

1. A Story About Me

Get child to express very basic facts about himself. Elicit name, age, school, and one other thing. Results will be a short, four-line story.

Example:

My name is Billy
I am four years old.
I come to school everyday.
I am a big boy.

Sample done by three-year old:

Brandt
I am "free" years old.
I don't go to school,
but I am a big boy.

2. A Story About My Family

After discussing that families are not always neat nuclear families, but those people closest to us that we live with and love, elicit names of family members and write a simple story in the child's words.

Example:

My name is Billy.
I have a mother.
I have a brother—his name is Jackie.
I have a sister—her name is Jeannie.

Sample done by three-year old:

Brandt
Michael—that's my brother.
My dad, my mom.
I don't have any more people.
Our kitty lives at my house.

3. A Story About How I Look

After discussing likenesses and differences such as size, hair color, skin color, etc. get child to give three facts about his appearance (or his perception of his appearance).

Sample done by four-year old:

My name is Billy.	I'm Billy.
I am big and strong.	I'm big and strong and
I have black hair.	I don't get hurt
My hair is curly.	'cause I'm bionic.

4. A Story About My School

Discuss favorite daily activities in school/day care center. Get child to tell you three things he does daily.

Example:

I come to school everyday.
We play outside.
We have cookies and milk.
The teacher reads stories.

5. A Story About Things I Like

Discuss briefly favorite foods, toys, pets, books, clothes. Then elicit three things the child likes very much.

Example:

I like my dog Sam best.
I like my bike.
I like pizza and ice cream.
I really like swimming in summer.

Try these and experiment with others—but always make the child's words and stories important. Let him take them home to show mother, make a book, a newsletter, mount them attractively, reread them with him, illustrate—do something to make them important.

More Language Development
To Correlate With Self-Concept

Creating little catchy couplets or rhymes with children's names is fun and it also helps sharpen and refine language skills. Of course some names are harder than others, but you can go to last names or use another word at the end of the line if necessary. Nonsense rhymes are most enjoyed. They really don't have to make sense, but they do have to be rhythmic and fun to say or chant.

Examples:

> Little Sue, with eyes of blue
> Works hard at all she can do.

> Mary, Mary, quite contrary
> She is not just ordinary.

> Billy Ray is just past three
> He's getting bigger as you can see.

> Joey Smith is so tall
> He's nearly high as a wall.

> Tim is learning how to swim
> A fish is what we now call him.

Self-Concept

SUGGESTED ART ACTIVITIES
TO CORRELATE WITH LANGUAGE TEACHING

1. Trace around child's whole body on newsprint or butcher paper. Have child fill in his clothes, facial features, etc. Write a story to accompany the picture.

2. Use child's handprint to make designs. Stress uniqueness of each person's finger prints. Tempera or finger paint can be used. Simple language experience stories can be dictated by child to accompany designs. Many interesting and colorful designs can be made. Let him experiment. See example below.

3. Make silhouettes of each child by taping a large piece of white construction paper on the wall. Shine a bright light (film strip projectors work fine) on paper. Have child stand in profile along side paper. Trace outline of shadow. Cut out and mount. These make nice gifts for Mother's Day.

4. Take pictures of each child. Let them mount them and have a language experience story displayed along with picture. They can also be very special valentines or Christmas cards for parents.

5. Have children draw pictures of their favorite toys and dictate a sentence or two about their picture.

6. Have children cut pictures of toys from magazines or catalogs and make collages of their favorites.

7. Use names as the basis for designs. Print very heavily with crayon, then fold over and press—color in letters in varied ways.

8. Names can be used other ways. Simply coloring in block letters, or cutting out construction paper letters in various shapes, as in the following examples, can be decorative and fun.

References

1. Durkin, Delores. *Children Who Read Early.* New York: Teacher's College Press, Columbia University, 1966.
2. Veatch, Jeanette et al. *Key Words to Reading: The Language Experience Approach Begins.* Columbus, Ohio: Charles E. Merrill Co., 1973.
3. Hymes, James L. Jr. *Teaching the Child Under Six.* Columbus, Ohio: Charles E. Merrill Co., 1974.
4. Piaget, Jean. "How Children Form Mathematical Concepts." In *Readings in the Psychology of Cognition,* edited by R.E. Anderon and D.P. Ansubel. New York: Holt, Rinehart and Winston, 1965.
5. Spodek, Bernard. *Teaching in the Early Years.* Englewood Cliffs, New Jersey: Prentice-Hall, Inc., 1978.
6. Fehr, Howard F. *This Is My Family.* New York: Holt, Rinehart and Winston, 1963.
7. Romey, William D. *Inquiry Techniques for Teaching Science.* Englewood Cliffs, New Jersey: Prentice-Hall, Inc., 1968.
8. Lowenfeld, Victor, and Brittain, W. Lambert. *Creative and Mental Growth.* New York: The Macmillan Publishing Co., Inc., 1970.
9. Seefeldt, Carol. *A Curriculum for Child Care Centers.* Columbus, Ohio: Charles E. Merrill Co., 1974.

SUPPLEMENTAL REFERENCES

1. Allen, Roach Van, and Allen, Claryce. *Language Experience in Early Childhood.* Chicago: Encyclopedia Britannica Press, 1964.
2. Auckerman, Robert C. *Approaches to Beginning Reading.* New York: John Wiley and Sons, 1971.
3. Corcoran, Gertrude B. *Language Experience for Nursery and Kindergarten Years.* Itasca, Illinois: F.E. Peacock Publishers, 1976.
4. Durkin, Delores. *Teaching Young Children to Read.* Boston, Mass.: Allyn and Bacon, Inc., 1976.
5. Mills, Belen C. *Understanding the Young Child and His Curriculum.* New York: The Macmillan Publishing Co., Inc., 1972.
6. Piaget, Jean. *The Child's Conception of Numbers.* New York: W.W. Norton, 1965.
7. Kellogg, Rhoda, with O'Dell, Scott. *The Psychology of Children's Art.* New York: Random House, 1967.
8. Hildebrand, Verna. *Introduction to Early Childhood Education.* New York: Macmillan Publishing Co., Inc., 1976.
9. Caldwell, Bettye M. Project Head Start: *Daily Program II—For a Child Development Center.* Washington, D.C.: Office of Economic Opportunity, 1968.
10. Moyer, J. *Bases for World Understanding and Cooperation.* Washington, D.C.: NEA/Association for Supervision and Curriculum Development, 1970.

THE CURRICULUM

Chapter 9

TRENDS IN
EARLY
CHILDHOOD
EDUCATION

Before any projections for the future are made it might be well to review briefly some of the basic material that has been presented.

Early childhood education currently includes all programs specifically designed for the young child from birth through age eight. This means programs such as Head Start, day care centers, preschools, nursery schools, as well as kindergartens and the primary grades in public and private schools. All these are included under the umbrella known as early childhood education.

Research has yielded much new knowledge about how children learn and the large amount of knowledge children acquire during these formative years. The acquisition of language and the mastery of language skills are particularly vital. Children must gain these language learnings early if they are to succeed in later school experiences. Remediation of language deficiencies becomes increasingly difficult as children become older.

There have been numerous compensatory programs developed for children in federally funded projects. Head Start and Follow Through have been instrumental in implementing these programs. A wide variety of models are presently being utilized.

The great interest in early childhood programs has developed not only because of research and experimental programs, but also because of major societal changes in our country. Changes in life style, working mothers, concern for providing equal opportunity for all, the effort to eliminate racism and sexism, and technological changes have all served to provide an impetus to early childhood education.

The curriculum for young children is often heavily weighted in favor of language activities, but it should be an integrated whole including all subject areas that are a part of any complete curriculum.

Teachers of young children have a vitally important role and there is new interest and concern about better preparing them.

With this background in mind, what does the future hold for early childhood education? There will almost certainly be more and better day care programs available. Massive child care bills have been rejected by presidential veto in recent years, but one was signed in 1975, indicating that government is ultimately going to become more responsive to the needs and wishes of working parents. The growth both in number and quality of day care centers seems inevitable.

Perhaps if the federal government does not respond adequately more will be done by state and local governments. Some states are already broadening their support of various types of early childhood programs. California, for example, is making early childhood education available to four-year olds in a number of its elementary schools. Other states, too, are expanding their public school offerings to include prekindergarten children.

With more early childhood programs of all types there will be more of a need for teacher preparation programs so that classrooms can be well-staffed with effective and competent teachers and aides.

One very new type of training is already available. The C.D.A. or Child Development Associate is already being prepared throughout the country, and this credential will undoubtedly receive more recognition in the future. The C.D.A. is given approximately two years of training in working with young children. It is a practical performance based preparation, with students spending most of their time actually working in early childhood learning situations. When students are deemed competent in a number of predetermined areas they are awarded the C.D.A. C.D.A.s work as assistant teachers in Head Start programs, day care centers, nursery schools, and other preschool programs.

There will also be a continuing need for fully certified professionals with undergraduate and graduate degrees. Most teacher education institutions have already felt this, and early childhood preparation programs are being expanded at all levels. There will be more concern shown by the public as society becomes more aware of the value and worth of early childhood education.

Laws pertaining to child abuse have not been discussed elsewhere and should receive attention. There is national concern about the problem of child abuse, and the definition has been expanded to cover physical *and* emotional damage inflicted on a child.

All fifty states have passed some type of protective legislation and most states now require that suspected cases of child abuse be reported by teachers to the police or the child protective agency in the county. Teachers are in a position to discover abuse more readily than many others in a community. If a child shows indication of physical abuse, nutritional neglect, medical care neglect, or sexual abuse it should be looked into and reported. In some cases severe neglect of hygiene should be reported. Serious emotional abuse or educational neglect should also be reported, although both of these are very difficult to substantiate. The reporting person's identity is protected in all fifty states.

These laws certainly have future implications for all parents and teachers of young children. They should improve life for countless children and permit them to live happier, more fulfilling lives with more successful school experiences.

Perhaps the most noteworthy new development in early childhood education and, in fact, for schools and educators generally, is Public Law 94-142, the Education for all Handicapped Children Act of 1975, which became law in November of 1975. However, it will take several years for it to be fully implemented. It is a very complex and all-encompassing piece of legislation which will inevitably have many far reaching consequence for all educators, and particularly those in early childhood education.

The purpose of this law is to ensure a free, appropriate, public education for all handicapped children, emphasizing special education and related services. This education will be individually designed to meet the unique needs of the handicapped child.

The following is a partial listing of what the federal law requires:

1. *Special Education:* free, specially designed instruction to meet the handicapped child's unique needs, including instruction in classrooms, homes, hospitals, and institutions.

2. *Related Services:* transportation and supportive services, including speech, audiology, psychological, physical and occupational therapy, recreation, and medical counseling, including identification and assessment.

3. *Individualized Educational Program* (IEP): a written statement developed by the local education association representatives, teacher, parents, and child (when appropriate) which must include:

   a. child's present level of educational performance
   b. annual goals and short term objectives
   c. specific educational services to be provided
   d. extent to which child will be able to participate in the regular classroom
   e. projected date for initiation and duration of services
   f. objective criteria and evaluation procedures
   g. schedule for determining if instructional objectives are being achieved (must be reviewed annually at least).

4. *Native Language:* the language normally used by the child or child's parents.

Implementing this law is going to be very expensive, and each state must develop a plan which meets all the criteria set in P.L. 94-142 for insuring that full educational opportunity is available to all handicapped children, that a detailed timetable is set for accomplishing goals, and that there is a description of the kind and number of facilities, personnel, and services necessary to meet goals. By September of 1978 each state must have provided this appropriate education for all handicapped children between ages three and eighteen. Some states have gone further and require that all these services be provided for ages birth through twenty-one. After all these children are located, the state must set priorities for services to the handicapped not receiving an education and to those with the most severe handicaps who may be receiving an inadequate education. Many procedural safeguards have been written into the law to be sure it is carried out as was intended.

All this indicates that early childhood education should continue to grow, and perhaps in the not too distant future we will have early childhood programs available for *all* children in our country who need and want them. There should be quality programs not just for the poor, the handicapped, or the most affluent segments of our society—but for all.

Annotated
Bibliography

Allen, Roach Van, and Allen, Claryce. *Language Experience in Early Childhood.* Chicago: Britannica, 1964. (A complete program of topics, lessons, and activities for preschool children based on language experiences)

Athey, I. J., and Rubadeau, N. J. *Educational Implications of Piaget's Theory: A Book of Readings.* Waltham, Mass.: Blaisdell Publications, 1971. (A fascinating collection of simplified interpretations of Piaget's work)

Atkinson, Carrol, and Maleska, Eugene T. *The Story of Education.* New York: Chilton Books, 1965. (A survey of educational history in encapsulated form)

Auckerman, Robert C. *Approaches to Beginning Reading.* New York: Wiley, 1971. (Current approaches to beginning reading concisely presented)

Baldwin, A. L. *Theories of Child Development.* New York: Wiley, 1968. (A useful description of varied child development theories used today)

Becker, Wesley, and Engleman, Siegfried. *University of Illinois Follow-Through Approach: The Systematic Use of Reinforcement Principles.* Urbana, Ill: Illinois University Press, 1968. (A rationale for the behavioristic approach used by Becker and Engleman in their early work)

Bereiter, Carl. *Acceleration of Intellectual Development in Early Childhood.* Urbana, Ill: Illinois University Press, 1967. (Bereiter presents principles utilized in the first Academic Preschool established by him and Engleman)

Bereiter, Carl, and Engleman, Siegfried. *Teaching the Disadvantaged Child.* Englewood Cliffs, N. J.: Prentice-Hall, 1966. (Again, the results of Bereiter' and Engleman's early experiences in designing direct, forceful instruction for culturally deprived children)

Blackie, J. *Inside the Primary School.* London, England: Her Majesty's Stationery Office, 1967. (Blackie discusses the changes in British elementary education leading to the informal, open approach.)

Bloom, Benjamin S. *Stability and Change in Human Characteristics.* New York: Wiley, 1964. (A massive definitive study of human intelligence and its development)

Braun, S. J., and Edwards, E. P. *History and Theory of Early Childhood Education.* Belmont, Cal.: Wadsworth, 1972. (A thorough and complete history of early childhood education)

Brophy, Jere E.; Good, Thomas L; and Nedler, Shari E. *Teaching in the Preschool.* New York: Harper and Row, 1975. (An overview of early childhood education with emphasis on the teacher and the learning environment)

Bruner, Jerome. *The Process of Education.* Cambridge, Mass.: Harvard University Press, 1960. (The work in which Bruner presents his famous theory of teaching any subject to any age—if properly done)

Bruner, J. S. et al. *Studies in Cognitive Growth.* New York: Wiley, 1966. (Bruner's research on intellectual development and learning stages)

Carter, Hugh, and Glick, Paul. *Marriage and Divorce.* Cambridge, Mass.: Harvard University Press, 1976. (Current information about the state of marriage, the family, and the current complexities of American family life)

Cave, William M., and Chesler, Mark A. *Sociology of Education.* New York: Macmillan, 1974. (An anthology of issues and problems in education)

Chow, Stanley H. L., and Elmore, Patricia. *Early Childhood Information Unit, Resource Manual and Program Descriptions.* Educational Products Information Exchange (EPIE) Institute, 1973. (An informative manual accompanying a multimedia kit on early childhood education programs)

Corcoran, Gertrude B. *Language Experience for Nursery and Kindergarten Years.* Itasca, Ill.: F. E. Peacock, 1976. (Describes what and how of language experiences for preschoolers including acquisition of language and activities to enhance it)

Deutsch, Martin et al. *The Disadvantaged Child.* New York: Basic Books, 1967. (An anthology by Deutsch and associates dealing with language, social class, and race, as they affect education)

Durkin, Delores. *Children Who Read Early.* New York: Teachers College Press, Columbia University, 1966. (Durkin describes the results of her research on children who read before school—who, how, and why.)

Durkin, Delores. *Teaching Young Children to Read.* Boston: Allyn and Bacon, 1976. (Durkin expands on her earlier research to discuss most appropriate ways of teaching early reading.)

Eliason, Carol F., and Jenkins, Loa T. *A Practical Guide to Early Childhood Education.* St. Louis, Mo: C. V. Mosby, 1977. (A helpful and practical guide to appropriate preschool curricular activities)

Evans, Ellis D. *Contemporary Influences in Early Childhood Education.* New York: Holt, Rinehart and Winston, 1971. (Evans reviews major influences such Piaget, Montessori, British Infant Schools, and key psychological approaches in early childhood education.)

Featherstone, J. *Schools Where Children Learn.* New York: Liveright, 1961. (Featherstone builds on his early study of British Infant School methods to encourage open education.)

Fehr, Howard F. *This Is My Family.* New York: Holt, Rinehart and Winston, 1963. (A children's book which presents simple mathematical concepts - sets, subsets)

Fisher, Dorothy C. *The Montessori Manual for Teachers and Parents.* Boston: Robert C. Bentley, 1964. (An avid disciple of Montessori, Fisher adapts many Montessori ideas for use with parents and teachers in non-Montessori schools.)

Flavell, J. *The Developmental Psychology of Jean Piaget.* Princeton, N. J.: Van Nostrand, 1963. (Flavell's readable interpretation of Piaget's developmental theory of psychology)

Frost, Joe L. *Early Childhood Education Rediscovered.* New York: Holt, Rinehart and Winston, 1968. (A book of rather important readings on all aspects of early childhood education)

————. *Revisiting Early Childhood Education.* New York: Holt, Rinehart and Winston, 1973. (Another excellent book of readings)

Frost, Joe L., and Kissinger, Joan B. *The Young Child and the Educative Process.* New York: Holt, Rinehart and Winston, 1976. (Provides a foundation of history, theory and philosophy of early childhood education)

Gesell, Arnold et al. *The First Five Years of Life.* New York: Harper and Row, 1940. (Gesell's classic study of children's behavior in their early years)

A Guide for Kindergarten Teachers. Sioux Falls Public Schools, S. D., current ed. (A curriculum guide developed by a local school district)

Hechinger, Fred M. *Pre-School Education Today.* New York: Doubleday, 1966. (Hechinger takes a critical look at the momentum generated by early childhood education in the sixties.)

Heimstra, Roger. *The Educative Community.* Lincoln, Neb.: Professional Educators Publications, 1972. (Sociological elements that go into making a successful educational system)

Hess, Robert D., and Croft, Doreen J. *Teachers of Young Children.* Boston: Houghton Mifflin, 1975. (An introductory book on all facets of early childhood education designed for teacher education)

Hildebrand, Verna. *Introduction to Early Childhood Education.* New York: Macmillan, 1976. (Hildebrand provides an excellent introductory book that covers curriculum and teaching style in early childhood education.)

Hipple, Marjorie L. *Early Childhood Education: Problems and Methods.* Pacific Palisades, Cal.: Goodyear, 1975. (Hipple presents a very readable case study approach to problems encountered in early childhood education.)

Howe, Louise K. *The Future of the Family.* New York: Simon and Schuster, 1972. (A look at parents, children, sex roles, and work as they relate to communities and day care)

Hunt, J. McV. *Intelligence and Experience.* New York: Ronald Press, 1961. (Hunt summarizes his findings that early intervention can increase intelligence.)

Hymes, James L. *Teaching the Child Under Six.* Columbus, Ohio: Charles A. Merrill, 1974. (Hymes presents his child-centered philosophy of early education along with the hope that all children and families can benefit from early education in the future.)

Kellogg, Rhoda, and O'Dell, Scott. *The Psychology of Children's Art.* New York: Random House, 1967. (Noted authority Kellogg presents, with O'Dell, her theory of child development through art in this lavishly illustrated book.)

King, Edith W., and Kerber, August. *The Sociology of Early Childhood Education.* New York: American Book, 1968. (A useful look at all facets of American society as it relates to early childhood education)

Lellard, Paula P. *Montessori, A Modern Approach.* New York: Schocken, 1972. (An updated version of Montessori's ideas and teaching approach)

Lowenfeld, Victor, and Brittain, W. Lambert. *Creative and Mental Growth.* New York: Macmillan, 1970. (Developmental stages as interpreted from children's art through research and observation)

Margolin, Edythe. *Sociocultural Elements of Early Childhood Education.* New York: Macmillan, 1974. (A study of the education of young children within the sociocultural context along with social problems related to curriculum)

—————. *Young Children: Their Curriculum and Learning Processes.* New York: Macmillan, 1976. (Margolin discusses curriculum within its conceptual framework.)

Milhollan, Frank, and Forisha, Bill E. *From Skinner to Rogers: Contrasting Approaches to Education.* Lincoln, Neb.: Professional Educators Publications, 1972. (A most concise explanation of humanistic psychology as opposed to behaviorism)

Mills, Belen C. *Understanding the Young Child and his Curriculum.* New York: Macmillan, 1972. (A collection of readings on the young child, social factors, and curriculum in the U. S. and other nations)

Montessori, Maria. *The Absorbent Mind.* New York: Dell, 1967. (Montessori presents her theory of providing the right sensory and language learning during the right sensitive period.)

Moyer, J. *Bases for World Understanding and Cooperation.* Washington, D. C.: NEA/Association for Supervision and Curriculum Development, 1970.

Piaget, Jean. *The Child's Conception of Number.* New York: W. W. Norton, 1965. (The child's rudimentary concept of numbers is explored in this treatise by Piaget.)

_____. *The Origins of Intelligence in Children.* New York: W. W. Norton, 1963. (Piaget's exposition of developmental learning based on his research and observation)

Pines, Maya. *Revolution in Learning: The Years from Birth to Six.* New York: Harper and Row, 1967. (A popularized version of early childhood education research and experimental programs of the sixties written to interest parents in children's potential)

Preschool Breakthrough: What Works in Early Childhood Education. Washington, D. C.: The National School Public Relations Associations, 1970. (A brief summary of research and programs from the experimental sixties)

Primary Education. London, England: Her Majesty's Stationery Office, 1959. (The official view of British primary education from the Ministry of Education)

Rich, John M. *Challenge and Response: Education in American Culture.* New York: Wiley, 1974. (An educational sociology text dealing with teachers and their role in society as well as the broader picture of education)

Robison, Helen F. *Exploring Teaching in Early Childhood Education.* Boston: Allyn and Bacon, 1977. (A broad look at early childhood education philosophy as well as specific program areas)

Romey, William D. *Inquiry Techniques for Teaching Science.* Englewood Cliffs, N.J.: Prentice-Hall, 1968. (This provides methods to encourage the inquiry approach in teaching science.)

Seefeldt, Carol. *A Curriculum for Child Care Centers.* Columbus, Ohio: Charles A. Merrill, 1974. (A practical and complete curriculum guide with many functional suggestions for day care staff)

Smart, Mollie S., and Smart, Russell C. *School Age Children.* New York: Macmillan, 1973. (One of several child development books by the Smarts which delineates characteristics of children at certain ages)

Spodek, Bernard. *Teaching in the Early Years.* Englewood Cliffs, N. J.: Prentice-Hall, 1978. (Spodek presents a complete and balanced early childhood education book for those in teacher education which includes an in depth coverage of curriculum.)

Standing, E. M. *Maria Montessori: Her Life and Work.* New York: New American Library, 1962. (Considered one of the most complete biographies of Montessori's life and theories)

Vance, Barbara. *Teaching the Prekindergarten Child: Instructional Design.* Monterey, Cal.: Brooks/Cole Publishing, 1973. (A curriculum book written from the behaviorist's point of view)

ANNOTATED BIBLIOGRAPHY

Veatch, Jeanette et al. *Key Words to Reading: The Language Experience Approach Begins.* Columbus, Ohio: Charles A. Merrill, 1973. (Veatch puts forth her language experience approach to beginning reading which is largely based on Ashton-Warner.)

Weber, Evelyn. *The Kindergarten: Its Encounter with Educational Thought in America.* New York: Teachers College Press, 1969. (A complete history of kindergarten through the sixties)

Weber, L. *The English Infant School and Informal Education.* Worthington, Ohio: Charles A. Jones, 1971. (The British Infant School—its rationale, theory, and practice—is presented.)

Weikart, D. *The Cognitively Oriented Curriculum: A Framework for Pre-School Teachers.* Washington, D. C.: National Association for the Education of Young Children, 1971. (Weikart describes his Piagetian curriculum and teaching methods in depth.)

Westinghouse Learning Corporation. *The Impact of Head Start: An Evaluation of the Effects of Head Start Experience on Children's Cognitive and Affective Development.* Athens, Ohio: Ohio University, 1969.

White, Burton L. *The First Three Years of Life.* Englewood Cliffs, N.J.: Prentice-Hall, 1975. (The results of White's extensive study of infants' abilities cover the educational potential of the child as well as developmental traits.)

Widmer, Emmy L. *The Critical Years: Early Childhood Education at the Crossroads.* Scranton, Penn.: International Textbook, 1970. (A total look at early childhood education including kindergarten and primary grades)

ARTICLES, BOOKLETS, ADDRESSES

Carro, Geraldine. "Who Says Our Children Never Had it So Good?" *Ladies' Home Journal,* July 1976.

Katz, Lillian. "The Young Child in Focus." Opening Address Presented to the National Conference of the Australian Preschool Association. Melbourne, Australia, May 1976. cited in ERIC.

Piaget, Jean. "How Children Form Mathematical Concepts." In *Readings in the Psychology of Cognition.* Edited by Anderdon, R. E. and Ansubel, D. P. New York: Holt, Rinehart and Winston, 1965.

"Research Report: The Productive Language Assessment Tasks." *Bulletin of the High/Scope Foundation,* no. 3. (Winter 1976).

Tunney, John Varick. "How Smart Do You Want Your Child to Be?" *McCall's,* October 1970.

Webster, Loraine. "A Danish Experience." *The Elementary School Journal,* April 1975.

GOVERNMENT PUBLICATIONS

Bronfenbrenner, Urie. *Is Early Intervention Effective.* Washington, D. C.: Office of Child Development, HEW, 1974.

Caldwell, Bettye M. *Project Head Start: Daily Program II—for a Child Development Center.* Washington, D. C.: Office of Economic Opportunity, 1968.

Follow Through, A Resource Guide to Sponsor Models and Materials. Washington, D. C.: Office of Education, HEW, 1976.

It Works: Pre-School Program in Compensatory Education. Washington, D. C.: Office of Education, HEW, 1968.

Karnes, Merle B. *Research and Development Program on Preschool Disadvantaged Children: Final Report.* Washington, D. C.: Office of Education, HEW, 1969.

Love, John B. et al. *National Home Start Evaluation: Final Report Findings and Implications.* Washington, D. C.: Office of Child Development, HEW, 1976.

Model Programs, Childhood Education, Appalachia Pre-School Education Program. Washington, D. C.: U. S. Government Printing Office, 1970.

Nevius, John B., and Filgo, Dorothy J. *Home Start Education: A Guideline for Content Areas.* Washington, D. C.: HEW, 1977.

Project Head Start. *Parent Involvement—A Workbook of Training Tips for Head Start Staff.* Washington, D. C.: HEW, 1968.

Statistical Abstract of the United States. U. S. Dept. of Commerce, Bureau of Census, 1975.

Willson, Victor L. et al. *Final Report Curriculum Revision Reports For St. Francis, Todd County and White River Schools.* ESEA Title I, University of South Dakota, 1976.

Index